Independent School District #487
Upsala, Minnesota 56384

IT'S EASY TO COOK
Favorite American Recipes

Also by Betty L. Torre:

THE COMPLETE BEGINNER'S GUIDE TO EVERYDAY ITALIAN COOKING

IT'S EASY TO COOK

Favorite American Recipes

BETTY L. TORRE

ILLUSTRATIONS BY CAROL INOUYE

DOUBLEDAY & COMPANY, INC.
GARDEN CITY, NEW YORK

Dedicated to my Mom,
Ethelyn Kuster Longnecker,
who taught me to love the kitchen

Library of Congress Cataloging in Publication Data

Torre, Betty L
  It's easy to cook.

  Includes index.
  SUMMARY: Discusses basic cooking techniques and offers recipes for lunches, dinners, desserts, and a variety of regional, international, and special holiday dishes.
  1. Cookery, American—Juvenile literature.
[1. Cookery, American] I. Inouye, Carol. II. Title.
TX715.T713   641.5
ISBN 0-385-11091-x Trade
    0-385-11092-8 Prebound
Library of Congress Catalog Card Number 76–2826

Text Copyright © 1977 by Betty L. Torre
Illustrations Copyright © 1977 by Carol Inouye
ALL RIGHTS RESERVED
PRINTED IN THE UNITED STATES OF AMERICA
FIRST EDITION

CONTENTS

INTRODUCTION: AMERICAN COOKERY   1
- *Before You Start to Cook*   3
- *Safety Rules*   3
- *Cooking with Wine*   4
- *Cooking without Wine*   4
- *Menu Planning*   4

REGIONAL DISHES   5

INTERNATIONAL DISHES   27

HOLIDAY DISHES   49

LUNCH AND SUPPER DISHES   77

DESSERTS   97

WHAT EVERY KITCHEN NEEDS   127

WEIGHTS AND MEASURES   129

GLOSSARY OF COOKING TERMS   130

INDEX   132

INTRODUCTION: AMERICAN COOKERY

American cooking has a long tradition which goes back to the Indians. To this day, American food wears the unmistakable stamp of these native Americans and their produce—corn, beans, and squash. Four widely used American dishes still bear Indian names. Pone and hominy are from the Algonquian tribes; succotash is from the Narraganset and pemmican from the Cree. The last was once widely used by early explorers and pioneer plainsmen; today it is called jerked beef or jerky.

The Indians made the really great American discovery—corn. Finding it growing as wild grass that had apparently originated in the southern Mexican highlands, Indians cultivated corn and gave the world one of its finest and most valuable foods. In their widely varying languages and dialects the Indians gave corn different names, but all of them meant the same, "our life." And corn was life to the first white settlers too. It provided the backbone of many true American recipes: hominy grits, corn fritters, corn pudding, corn soup with egg dumplings, Indian pudding, spoon bread, johnnycake, and cornmeal pancakes.

In Colonial days, resourceful settlers put their ingenuity to work finding more and more ways to use the variety of meat, game, vegetables and fruits found in this country. In the wilds there were fruits and berries to be eaten fresh-picked or stewed or dried or made into jams, jellies, wines, or cordials. A wild orange grew in Florida. Honey was a source of sweetness. Our native American tree, the sugar maple, provided another source. A great supply of nuts—chestnuts, hickory, black walnuts, beechnuts, and acorns—was found in the forests.

Settlers from other lands brought their own native recipes with them—the Scotch and Irish their good hot breads, the English their meat pies and steamed puddings, the French their sauces and sweets, the Italians their pastas, the Dutch and Germans their hearty dumplings and stews, the Spanish their exotic delicacies, and the Scandinavians their smorgasbord.

Gradually these recipes have been swapped around, adapted to materials and ingredients at hand, and combined with what experience had already taught cooks of this country. Today these foods which originated in Europe, Africa, Asia, Canada, and Mexico are a significant part of our culinary heritage.

This melting pot of old and new has resulted in a noble repertoire of food. The combination of Old World foods and native American foods brought about a distinctive new cuisine. For example, cioppino is an American refinement of an Italian fish stew; chop suey was developed by Chinese-Americans; and fried chicken, sweet potato pie, and strawberry shortcake are American classics that have a found place beside the world's best dishes.

Today each section of America still enjoys the traditional foods peculiar to its vicinity. But modern transportation allows these foods to add variety and pleasure to Americans dining in every part of the United States. In the following pages you will find the traditional dishes of Pilgrim New England, the hearty country fare of the Midwest, the distinctive foods of the South, and the flavorful, informal favorites of the Southwest and West.

◆ BEFORE YOU START TO COOK ◆

1. **Read the entire recipe carefully first** so you will know what kind of cooking is involved, what utensils and what ingredients will be needed.
2. **Utensils:** get the large ones out—mixer, bowls, and pots.
3. **Ingredients:** get them together on the counter.
4. **Prepare the ingredients** as much as possible in advance.
5. **Follow each step of the directions exactly.** Remember that even the most complex dish is still prepared one step at a time. And each step in itself is simple.

◆ SAFETY RULES ◆

There are four basic safety rules which should be followed in the kitchen.

1. Slice, dice, chop, and mince on a chopping board.
2. When you use the vegetable peeler, cut away from yourself.
3. Always use pot holders on hot pans.
4. Pans won't upset and spill if the handles are turned to the back of the stove.

◈ COOKING WITH WINE ◈

More Americans are cooking today with wine to enhance the flavor and aroma of dishes. The alcohol cooks out, so there is no question of the food being intoxicating—except to your sense of smell and taste. Any wine you use for cooking should be a good one, as the flavor exaggerates after cooking. This doesn't mean that it must be an expensive vintage bottle, but it must be full of natural flavor.

◈ COOKING WITHOUT WINE ◈

There is no substitute for the flavor of wine, but if you prefer not to use it, simply omit it whenever it appears in a recipe. If you need more liquid, use beef or chicken bouillon or fish stock for main dishes, and usually orange juice or cider for desserts.

◈ MENU PLANNING ◈

To help you plan a complete meal, suggested menus have been included in this book. Recipes from the book have been used whenever possible. Page numbers of recipes contained elsewhere in this book are noted for your convenience.

REGIONAL DISHES

◆ NEW ENGLAND COOKERY ◆

Traditional New England cooking is hearty fare, simply prepared in the style used since Colonial times. Settlers learned quickly from Indians about corn, squash, pumpkins, codfish, clams, oysters, and lobsters; how to use herring to fertilize the corn hills; what greens and berries were edible; how to make spruce tea to ward off scurvy; and how to tap the maple trees and boil down sap for sweetening. It was here in New England that the feast day that has come down to us as Thanksgiving was begun.

BOSTON BAKED BEANS

Preparation and Cooking Time: 7 hours   *Serves 4–6*
(Does not include time to soak beans.)

It is for baked beans that Boston is known as Bean Town. The Puritan sabbath lasted from sundown on Saturday until sundown on Sunday. The bean pot could be kept in the slow heat of a fireplace to serve on Saturday and Sunday.

INGREDIENTS
2 cups (1 pound) dried navy or pea beans, washed and sorted
6 cups water

DIRECTIONS
Wash beans, discarding imperfect ones.

Cover beans with cold water and soak overnight.

Next day, place beans and enough water to cover in a large pot.

Bring to a boil and cook 2 minutes.
Reduce heat and simmer, covered, 30 minutes.
Drain beans, reserving cooking liquid.

Preheat oven to 300° F.

¼ *pound salt pork with rind*
1 medium onion

Cut off a ¼-inch slice of salt pork.
Place with onion in the bottom of a 2-quart bean pot.
Cut through rind of remaining salt pork every half inch, making 1-inch cuts.
Add beans to pot and bury salt pork in them.

½ *cup light molasses*
2 tablespoons brown sugar
½ *teaspoon powdered mustard*
1 teaspoon salt

Mix molasses, brown sugar, mustard, and salt together.
Heat reserved bean liquid to boiling point; stir 1 cup bean liquid into molasses mixture.
Pour over beans and add enough bean liquid or water to cover beans.

Cover bean pot and bake 6 hours or until done.
Add water as needed. Uncover for the last half hour of cooking so that the rind becomes brown and crisp.

NEW ENGLAND SUPPER
Boston Baked Beans
Boston Brown Bread (page 123)
___
Rice Pudding (page 99)

NEW ENGLAND CLAM CHOWDER

Preparation and Cooking Time: 30 minutes   *Serves 4*

A chowder is a thick, hearty soup that probably originated in New England. The most famous of the American chowders is clam chowder.

INGREDIENTS	DIRECTIONS
¼ pound lean salt pork, diced	Fry salt pork in a large pot until golden; remove and reserve. Drain off all but 3 tablespoons fat.
1 medium onion, diced	Add onion and sauté until limp and golden.
1 6-ounce bottle clam juice 2 medium potatoes, peeled and diced ½ teaspoon salt ⅛ teaspoon white pepper	Add clam juice, potatoes, salt and pepper; simmer until potatoes are tender, about 15 minutes.
2 8-ounce cans minced clams, undrained	Add clams and juice; cook until heated.

1 cup light cream, at room temperature	Slowly add cream, milk, and butter, stirring constantly.
1 cup milk, at room temperature	
1 tablespoon butter	Reheat but do not boil.
Paprika or chopped parsley	Top with reserved bits of crisp pork and paprika or chopped parsley for color. Serve at once.

CODFISH CAKES

Preparation and Cooking Time: 20 minutes   Serves 4
(*Does not include time for boiling fish and potatoes or chilling time.*)

Cod was once one of the main sources of food for New England. As early as 1640, the cod-fishing industry had reached such proportions that in one year New Englanders prepared 300,000 codfish for market. So important was the fish that a memorial to the codfish can be found in the Massachusetts House of Representatives.

INGREDIENTS	DIRECTIONS
2 cups cooked flaked codfish or other firm-bodied white fish	Combine fish, potatoes, onion, parsley, and butter together in a large bowl.
2 cups mashed potatoes	Add milk and mix together.
2 teaspoons minced onion	Then add eggs one at a time.
¼ cup minced fresh parsley	Mixture should not be too loose or cakes will fall apart when fried.
3 tablespoons butter, at room temperature	
½ cup milk	Shape into small, round, flat cakes or balls.
3 medium eggs, beaten	

Dry seasoned bread crumbs   Roll in bread crumbs and chill thoroughly before frying.

Oil for frying   Heat at least ¼ inch of oil in a heavy frying pan.
When hot, add cakes; cook, turning once, over a medium heat until nicely browned.
Drain on absorbent paper before serving.

NEW ENGLAND SUPPER

Clam Chowder

Codfish Cakes

Celery   Bread-and-Butter Pickles

Blueberry Muffins (page 126)

Bread Pudding (page 100)

PENNSYLVANIA
◆ DUTCH COOKERY ◆

Eating is serious business in Pennsylvania Dutch country—that fertile and lovely region in southeastern Pennsylvania. This is the land of scrapple, Philadelphia pepper pot soup, sauerkraut, schnitz un knepp (dried apples, ham, and dumplings cooked together), buckwheat cakes, shoofly pie, crisp funnel cakes (fried cakes), homemade noodles, and chicken pie.

Pennsylvania Dutch cooking is as popular today as it was during early American days when Presidents George Washington and James Buchanan favored Pennsylvania Dutch specialties.

SCHNITZ UN KNEPP
Dried Apples, Ham, and Dumplings

Preparation and Cooking Time: 3 hours 30 minutes   Serves 6

Schnitz means "cut," and in Pennsylvania Dutch usage, it has come to mean cut, dried apples.

INGREDIENTS	DIRECTIONS
1 3-pound smoked ham Water to cover	Place ham and enough water to cover it in a large pot; bring to a boil. Lower heat; cover and simmer 2 hours. Add more water if necessary.
4 cups dried apples Water to cover	Soak apples in water while ham is cooking. When ham has cooked 2 hours, add apples and water in which they have been soaking. Cook covered 1 hour or until apples are tender.
1 tablespoon brown sugar 1 cup raisins	Stir in brown sugar and raisins when apples are soft; bring to a gentle boil.

TO MAKE DUMPLINGS

2 cups flour
4 teaspoons baking powder
⅛ teaspoon freshly ground
    black pepper
1 teaspoon salt

Sift dry ingredients together in a large mixing bowl.

1 large egg, beaten
3 tablespoons melted butter
1 tablespoon milk,
    approximately

Beat together egg, melted butter, and milk; mix with flour mixture.
Batter should be slightly stiff. Add a bit more milk if necessary.
Drop by spoonfuls into boiling broth; cover and simmer without lifting lid for 20 minutes.
Serve when done.

PENNSYLVANIA DUTCH DINNER
Schnitz Un Knepp
Cauliflower Pickles
Green Bean Salad

Nobby Apple Cake (page 119)

◆ SOUTHERN COOKING ◆

Southern cooking is not uniform and never has been. It has been shaped by the abundance of local products—fruits and vegetables, fish and game—and the varied peoples who made the South their home. Probably the most important factor which gave distinction to southern cooking was the influence of African slaves, who had original ideas about seasoning and produced many culinary masterpieces.

If there is one place where Southern cooks outdo themselves it is in the dessert department. Peaches and strawberries, peanuts and pecans, sweet potatoes and yams are stirred into too-good-to-be-true shortcakes, puddings, and pies. Cake making is an art indulged in by southern cooks to produce rich chocolate cakes, layered jelly cakes, gold cakes, spice cakes, sponge cakes, hickory cakes, pound cakes and fruit cakes.

HAM HOCKS AND COLLARD GREENS

Preparation and Cooking Time: 3 hours *Serves 4*

Soul food, like jazz, was first created in the South by American blacks. All soul food is southern, but not all southern food is soul. Soul food means only those foods that blacks grew up eating at home.

INGREDIENTS
4 ham hocks
  or ½ pound salt pork
2 quarts water

DIRECTIONS
Place ham hocks or salt pork in a large pot with water.

(NOTE: Although one ham hock is enough for flavoring, put in one for each person you plan to serve if possible—especially if this is the main course.)

Bring to a boil; lower heat and simmer gently, covered, for 1 hour.

4 pounds fresh collard greens, cleaned and washed

Meanwhile wash and clean the collard greens; remove any coarse old leaves, tough stems, and midribs of leaves. Wash a second time under cold running water, as collard greens, like spinach, tend to be gritty. Drain.

After ham hocks have cooked for an hour, add greens.

Cover pot tightly and cook over *very* low heat for 2 hours or until ham hocks are fork tender.

Stir occasionally.

Salt and pepper to taste

Taste before adding salt and pepper.

The ham or salt pork usually gives sufficient flavoring.

VARIATIONS

Another time prepare this recipe using kale, beet, chard, turnip, or mustard greens. The cooking liquid is called "pot liquor." If used as a side dish, serve with ham and sweet potatoes.

SOUL FOOD SUPPER
Ham Hocks and Collard Greens
Hoe Cakes (page 124) or Corn Muffins

Rice Pudding (page 99)
Coffee

BRUNSWICK STEW

Preparation and Cooking Time: 2 hours *Serves 6–8*

This famous southern dish (Brunswick, Virginia, lays claim to it) was one of the principal attractions of political rallies, cockfights, family reunions, and other early Virginian gatherings. Originally made with squirrel, it can be varied and increased by adding other vegetables, pork spareribs, or stewing beef.

INGREDIENTS	DIRECTIONS
1 4-pound stewing chicken, cut up 1 teaspoon salt ¼ cup butter or margarine 2 medium onions, sliced	Sprinkle chicken with salt; sauté chicken and onions in melted butter in a large pot until lightly browned.

1 17-ounce can tomatoes
1 6-ounce can tomato paste
2 cups chicken broth
1 cup finely diced celery with leaves
¼ teaspoon marjoram
¼ teaspoon thyme
⅛ teaspoon oregano
⅛ teaspoon cayenne pepper
2 teaspoons salt

Stir in tomatoes, tomato paste, broth, celery, marjoram, thyme, oregano, cayenne pepper, and salt; cover and simmer 1 hour.

1 medium package frozen corn, thawed and drained
1 medium package frozen lima beans, thawed and drained

Add corn and lima beans; cook 20 minutes longer.

3 tablespoons butter
2 tablespoons flour

Melt butter in a small pan; blend in flour to make a roux.
Add a little liquid from stew, stirring until smooth; blend into stew and cook 2 minutes before serving.

SOUTHERN SUPPER
Brunswick Stew
Hoe Cakes (page 124)

Lemon Chess Pie (page 111)

◈ CREOLE COOKERY ◈

Creole cooking is a combination of classic French, Spanish, African, and Anglo-Saxon food spiced and seasoned with ingredients used by the local Choctaw and Chickasaw Indians. Gourmets from every part of the world come to its hometown, New Orleans. Most probably, Creole cooking is America's most original contribution to good food. This economical, subtle, exotic, and succulent cuisine certainly ranks with the finest in the world.

The dishes most closely associated with Creole cookery are the gumbos and the jambalayas, which are made with the wealth of seafood abundant in this area.

JAMBALAYA

Preparation and Cooking Time: 1 hour   *Serves 4*

Jambalaya (derived from the Spanish word *jamon* meaning ham) was introduced to New Orleans by the Spanish in the late 1700s. Creole cooks added shrimp. It is considered one of the classic Creole dishes.

INGREDIENTS	DIRECTIONS
¼ cup diced salt pork, or 3 slices bacon, diced, or 2 tablespoons butter	Cook salt pork or bacon until rendered of its fat in a large skillet.
1 large green pepper, diced 1 large onion, chopped 1 garlic clove, minced	Add green pepper, onion, and garlic, and sauté until onion is limp and golden.

1½ cups diced, cooked ham
2½ cups canned tomatoes, undrained
½ cup water
1 tablespoon minced fresh parsley or 1 teaspoon dried parsley
½ teaspoon thyme
1 teaspoon salt
⅛ teaspoon freshly ground black pepper
Pinch of cayenne pepper (opt.)

Add ham, tomatoes, water, parsley, thyme, salt and black pepper. Bring to a boil.

¾ cup uncooked rice
2 cups fresh shrimp, shelled, deveined and washed, or 2 cups frozen shrimp, thawed and drained

Add rice and shrimp to boiling broth; reduce heat and simmer, covered, over low heat 30 minutes or until rice is tender and most of the liquid has been absorbed. Add more water if dish becomes too dry.

NEW ORLEANS DINNER
Fresh Fruit Cup

Jambalaya
Chilled Green Beans with Oil and Vinegar

Lemon Sherbet
Coffee

◈ MIDWESTERN COOKERY ◈

The Midwest, land of lyrical Indian name states—Ohio . . . Iowa . . . Michigan . . . Minnesota . . . Nebraska—produces good, wholesome food descended from pioneer days. There are two important aspects to food in the Midwest. One is the grain—corn, wheat, soy beans, and oats—that grows in abundance on this fertile farm land, and the other is the cattle that are fed with it. There is no finer meal than a superb steak or a roast served with sweet corn picked minutes before cooking. The abundant wealth of raw materials is still further enriched by the varied culinary traditions of the people who settled this section. Flour from the grain is made into Scandinavian rye bread, Norwegian potato bread, Dutch fritters, German tortes, and an endless list of pies, cakes, and cookies. This is apple country. Apples team up with meats or are tucked into breads, dumplings, cobblers, and the ever-present pies. All this is sturdy fare which evokes fond memories of America's early days.

CHICKEN WITH HERBED DUMPLINGS

Preparation and Cooking Time: 2 hours 30 minutes

Serves 4–6

Fluffy dumplings with a hint of parsley, celery, and onion are delicious with stewed chicken.

INGREDIENTS	DIRECTIONS
1 4-pound chicken, cut up	Put chicken, water, salt,
1 quart water	carrots, onion, and celery in
2 teaspoons salt	a large enamel soup pot

2 carrots, sliced
1 onion, chopped
1 stalk of celery with leaves, chopped

(use a large kettle to allow for the swelling of dumplings); cook, covered, 1½ hours or until chicken is fork tender.
Remove chicken from broth; set aside and keep hot.
Strain stock, adding water if needed to make 3 cups.

⅓ cup flour
1 teaspoon paprika
1 cup milk

Combine flour, paprika, and milk until blended; add milk mixture slowly to broth, stirring constantly.
Return chicken to pot and heat 5 minutes.

TO MAKE DUMPLINGS

2 cups biscuit mix
¾ cup milk
1 tablespoon fresh minced parsley or 1 teaspoon dried parsley
½ teaspoon celery seeds
½ teaspoon instant minced onion

Combine biscuit mix, milk, parsley, celery seeds, and minced onion; drop from a tablespoon into boiling stock.
Lower heat. Cook, uncovered, over low heat in liquid that is just simmering for 10 minutes; cover and cook 10 minutes longer.
Serve with mashed potatoes.

MIDWESTERN DINNER
Chicken with Herbed Dumplings
Mashed Potatoes
Buttered Squash
Cranberry-Orange Relish (page 73)

Strawberry Shortcake (page 112)

◈SOUTHWESTERN COOKERY◈

Southwesterners are heirs to a unique combination of culinary traditions: Indian, Spanish, Mexican, Southwest cowboy and Anglo, or English. Southwesterners who regard the land as their life live and eat out of doors a great deal—barbecuing, cooking out, picnicking and backpacking. Here barbecues mean just one thing—beef, usually huge steaks simply seasoned. Still popular today are the flat cakes of corn called tortillas and an appetizer called guacamolé—puréed avocado with spicy seasonings—both of which the Spaniards learned from the Aztecs and then taught to Indians of the Southwest. Of the three sisters of Indian agriculture—corn, beans, and squash—beans are the darling in the Southwest. Everyone eats beans, especially refried beans. The Southwest has been pie-eating country ever since pie was the favorite dessert of the hard-working cowboys, who nicknamed their chuck-wagons "pie boxes." Fresh fruits finish every meal here.

TOSTADOS

Preparation and Cooking Time: 1 hour 30 minutes   Serves 4–6

A complete meal-in-one. Salad, refried beans, and chili are served together on flat tortillas. Mrs. Richard (Muriel) Levin uses convenience foods to take the work out of preparing this classic of the Southwest.

INGREDIENTS

TO MAKE MEAT BASE

1 pound ground beef
1 large onion, chopped
2 garlic cloves, chopped
½ teaspoon salt
⅛ teaspoon freshly ground black pepper

1 8-ounce can tomato sauce
1 6-ounce can tomato paste
1½ 6-ounce cans water
1 teaspoon or to taste chili powder
1 teaspoon oregano
1 teaspoon cumin seed

TO MAKE BEANS

1 16-ounce can refried plain beans
1 15½-ounce can refried beans with chorizo
Lard or bacon fat

TO MAKE CONDIMENTS

½ pound Jack or a mild

DIRECTIONS

Mix together ground beef, onion, garlic, salt and black pepper.
Place in a large skillet and sauté until well browned. Stir frequently.

Add tomato sauce, tomato paste, water, chili powder, oregano, and cumin seed.
Mix together to blend.
Simmer over low heat 1 hour. Stir occasionally. Serve hot.

Cook in a separate saucepan the beans in the lard or bacon fat until steaming. Turn frequently so they don't stick.

The condiments can be

Cheddar cheese, grated into tiny strips
2 cups shredded iceberg lettuce
1 cup chopped tomatoes
1 cup chopped scallions
1 cup sour cream
1 large avocado, peeled and chopped
1 tablespoon lemon juice

1 box of 12 open-face tostados
1 8-ounce bottle of mild or hot taco sauce

prepared earlier in the day as can everything else. The exact amount can be dependent upon what you have in the house. Grate the cheese on the side of the cheese grater with the big holes. Place each of the condiments in a separate bowl and arrange on a tray together. Sprinkle avocado with lemon juice to prevent darkening.

When ready to serve, heat tostados in oven until warm. To make tostados have your guests put together in roughly this order: on top of the tostado put refried beans, grated cheese, meat sauce, lettuce, tomatoes, scallions, sour cream, avocado, and either a mild or hot taco sauce.

SOUTHWESTERN DINNER
Tostados

Iced Pineapple
Coconut-Butter Cookies (page 103)
Coffee

◆ WESTERN COOKERY ◆

The Pacific coast—California, Oregon, and Washington—has its own traditional cuisine that began with the settlement of the Spaniards in the late 1700s. The West is blessed with an ocean of seafood, orchards of avocados and citrus fruits, vineyards of grapes, farm lands overflowing with vegetables and salad greens. Salads, in fact, are the West's great specialty—green salads, fruit salads, vegetable salads, meat and fish salads. Crab salad has become a world-famous classic. All over the Pacific coast there is a deep-rooted fondness for barbecues, evocative of pioneer days. The earliest European settlers in the Northwest found Indians roasting split salmon over open fires, and that still is a favorite method of cooking these magnificent fish.

CIOPPINO

Preparation and Cooking Time: 1 hour *Serves 4–6*

This delectable fish stew is one of California's great contributions to American cooking.

INGREDIENTS

4 tablespoons olive oil or butter
2 garlic cloves, minced
3 medium onions, chopped
1 medium green pepper, seeded and chopped

1 2-pound 3-ounce can Italian plum tomatoes, undrained

DIRECTIONS

Heat olive oil in an enamel soup pot; sauté garlic, onions, and green pepper in oil until the onion is limp and golden. Stir occasionally.

Add tomatoes, clam juice, clams, burgundy, oregano, basil, salt, and bay leaf to

2 cups clam juice
1 8-ounce can minced
   clams, undrained
1 cup burgundy
1 teaspoon oregano
½ teaspoon basil
½ teaspoon salt
1 bay leaf

1 pound halibut, sea bass, or
   any firm-bodied fish,
   cleaned and cut in chunks
1 pound raw shrimp, shelled
   (*leaving tails on*) and
   deveined
2 dozen fresh clams, well
   scrubbed

pot; cover and simmer 15 minutes.

Buy seafood already cleaned at the fish store or clean it yourself while broth is cooking.
Cut fish into chunks. Set aside.
To clean shrimp, shell, leaving the tails on; split each shrimp down the back and remove the black intestinal vein.
Wash in cold water; set aside.
Scrub clams with a stiff brush to remove sand; rinse in cold water at least three times.
When broth has simmered, add fish and cook covered 5 minutes.
Add shrimp and cook covered 5 minutes.
Add clams; cover and cook 10 minutes longer or until clams open and shrimps turn pink.
Correct seasoning if necessary.

Serve hot with crusty sourdough bread.

VARIATIONS

This recipe can be doubled easily using whatever seafood is available. Crab, lobster, mussels or oysters are happy additions.
It can also be made with just shellfish.
The stew can be prepared ahead, but add the fish and shellfish just before serving.

WESTERN DINNER
Cioppino
**Sourdough Bread
or Italian Bread Sticks**

**Fresh Pears and Cheese
Espresso**

INTERNATIONAL DISHES

There are certain "foreign" dishes which have become such favorites in this country that they represent a unique part of American cooking. For example, spaghetti with meatballs or meat sauce is one of the top ten most popular dishes in the United States today. Pasta was always made by Americans of Italian ancestry, but today everybody makes spaghetti or sauerbraten or gazpacho or other strictly ethnic dishes. Here are a few of the best-known recipes which are made so often that they seem to belong in any collection of basic American favorites.

◈ ENGLAND ◈

SHEPHERD'S PIE

Preparation and Cooking Time: 1 hour   *Serves 4–6*

This is a favorite English supper that has found its way to the American table.

INGREDIENTS	DIRECTIONS
TO MAKE MASHED POTATOES	
4 medium potatoes, peeled and quartered	Place potatoes in pot with enough water to cover.
Water to cover	(NOTE: Many cooks prefer to cook potatoes in their skins and peel afterward.)
	Bring to a boil; lower heat, cover and cook until tender, about 15–20 minutes; then drain.

3 tablespoons butter, at room temperature
6 tablespoons heavy cream or milk (approximately)
Salt and black pepper to taste

With a potato masher or electric mixer, mash potatoes thoroughly until no lumps remain. Add butter and cream; beat until fluffy. Season to taste with salt and black pepper.
Keep warm.

TO MAKE PIE

1 large onion, finely chopped
2 tablespoons butter

Preheat oven to 400°F.
Grease 1½-quart shallow casserole or a deep pie plate. Set aside.
Sauté onion in butter in large skillet until limp and golden.

2½ cups cooked roast beef, lamb, veal, or pork, minced
1 tablespoon flour

Sprinkle meat with flour; add to pan and brown lightly on all sides.

2½ cups beef gravy
2 teaspoons Worcestershire sauce
1 tablespoon minced fresh parsley
¼ teaspoon thyme
Salt and freshly ground black pepper to taste

Add gravy, Worcestershire sauce, parsley, thyme, salt and black pepper to taste.
Heat and then pour into greased dish.

1 large egg, beaten
½ cup grated mild Cheddar cheese

Fold egg and cheese into warm mashed potatoes.
Arrange in ring on top of meat.

Bake until gravy bubbles and potato ring is light golden brown, about 15–20 minutes.

VARIATIONS

Instead of meat, use leftover cooked fish in a cream sauce.

Add small canned onions, cooked carrots, or cooked mushrooms.

ENGLISH SUPPER
Shepherd's Pie
Mixed Pickles
Rolls   Butter
―――
Trifle (page 114)
Tea

◈ FRANCE ◈

HAM AND ASPARAGUS SOUFFLÉ

Preparation and Cooking Time: 1 hour   *Serves 4*

Soufflés are not that difficult to make, and they are a marvelous way to use up leftovers.

INGREDIENTS	DIRECTIONS
	Preheat oven to 400° F.
1 cup cooked, diced asparagus	Place asparagus in the bottom of an ungreased 1½-quart straight-sided casserole. Set aside.
3 tablespoons butter ¼ cup flour 1 cup milk, heated	Melt butter in top of double boiler; stir in flour until well mixed. Add heated milk a little at a time; cook, stirring constantly, over boiling water until smooth and thick.
¼ cup sharp Cheddar cheese, grated ½ teaspoon salt 1 teaspoon dry mustard	Add grated cheese, salt, and dry mustard; stir until smooth and creamy. Remove from heat and cool slightly.
4 egg yolks, beaten	Stir a little cheese sauce into beaten egg yolks; slowly stir this mixture into rest of cheese sauce.
4 egg whites, beaten until stiff but not dry ½ cup ground, cooked ham	Beat egg whites until stiff. Fold egg whites and ham into cheese sauce; pour into casserole. Mixture should not reach the top of the dish. To form a crown, make a shallow path with edge of a knife about 1 inch from

edge of the dish all the way around.
Bake uncovered for 5 minutes.
Lower heat to 375° F. and continue baking for 30 minutes or until golden.

FRENCH SUPPER
Ham and Asparagus Soufflé
Romaine Salad
Bread Sticks

Fresh Fruit Compote

═══════════════════════════

◈ GERMANY ◈

SAUERBRATEN

Preparation and Cooking Time: 2 hours 30 minutes
Serves 4–6
(*Does not include marinating time.*)

Sauerbraten with gingersnap gravy and potato dumplings is probably the best known and loved of the German dishes in this country. Mrs. Freida Petsche brought this recipe with her from Germany.

INGREDIENTS

2–3 pounds beef (chuck, rump, or round)
Salt and pepper

1 cup vinegar
1 cup water
2 bay leaves
6 peppercorns
2 cloves

1 tablespoon oil
3 carrots, cut into strips
3 onions, sliced

1½ teaspoons sugar
6 gingersnaps

DIRECTIONS

Sprinkle meat thoroughly with salt and pepper.
Place in an earthen dish.

Add vinegar, water, bay leaves, peppercorns, and cloves; let stand tightly covered in a cool place for 2–3 days.
Turn meat in marinade occasionally.

Drain meat, reserving liquid.
Heat oil in Dutch oven; brown meat in hot oil on all sides.
Add carrots, onions, and 1 cup of the spiced vinegar mixture.
Cover and cook over low heat 2 hours or until meat is tender.

When meat is cooked, add sugar and crumbled gingersnaps; cook 10 minutes more.
This makes a delicious gravy.
Add more spiced vinegar mixture if necessary.

VARIATIONS

Omit gingersnaps and thicken gravy with flour moistened with water.

POTATO DUMPLINGS

Preparation and Cooking Time: 45 minutes   *Serves 4–6*

Dumplings should be light and fluffy. Farina is the secret ingredient.

INGREDIENTS
5 medium potatoes
Water to cover

½ teaspoon salt
2 medium eggs
½ cup flour
⅓ cup farina or bread crumbs
¼ teaspoon nutmeg

Boiling salted water

DIRECTIONS
Boil potatoes in their jackets until tender; remove skins and press through a food ricer.
Allow to cool slightly.

Add salt, 1 egg, flour, farina, and nutmeg. Mix thoroughly.
Add another egg if mixture is too dry or more farina if mixture is too moist.
Form mixture into balls about size of a walnut.
Drop balls into boiling salted water.
When balls come to surface, boil uncovered for 3 minutes.
Remove one from liquid and cut open; if center is dry, they are cooked.
Remove from liquid. Serve immediately with sauerbraten and gingersnap gravy.

GERMAN DINNER
Sauerbraten with Gingersnap Gravy
Potato Dumplings
Sweet-sour Red Cabbage
Pumpernickel Bread   Butter
———
Apple Pie (page 107)
Coffee

❖ SCANDINAVIA ❖

SWEDISH MEAT BALLS

Preparation and Cooking Time: 1 hour 15 minutes
Makes 100 meat balls approximately

Sweden, Denmark, and Norway have all contributed to Scandinavia's sumptuous buffet meal known as smorgasbord. Guests come to the table three times—for appetizers, meats, and desserts. Mrs. Lou (Joanne) Starkey shares her grandmother's recipe for Swedish meat balls.

INGREDIENTS	DIRECTIONS
6 slices stale white bread	Soak bread in water in a bowl.
Water to cover	Squeeze the water out of the bread with your fingers and break up the bread in a mixing bowl.

3 medium onions
3 pounds ground pork
1½ teaspoons salt
¼ teaspoon freshly ground black pepper

Grate the onions directly into the mixing bowl so as not to lose the juice.

Mix the onion-bread mixture with the pork, salt, and black pepper until thoroughly blended. Season to taste.

Wet hands in cold water before forming meat mixture into tiny meat balls about the size of a large marble.

Brown meat balls a few at a time in a large skillet. Drain on absorbent paper.

Place browned meat balls in a heavy Dutch oven or a large deep skillet with a cover.

½ cup water

Add ½ cup water; simmer covered over low heat for 45 minutes or until pork is well cooked. Add more water if necessary.

Serve with boiled parsleyed potatoes.

VARIATIONS

Leftovers make great sandwiches or make into a meat ball Stroganoff.

Sauté 2 tablespoons minced onion in butter; add meat balls and canned mushrooms. When heated, add 1 cup sour cream. Season and serve with rice or noodles.

SCANDINAVIAN SMORGASBORD
Tiny Open-faced Sandwiches
***
Swedish Meat Balls
Ham   Baked Beans (page 6)
Boiled Potatoes with Dill
Cabbage Salad   Pickled Beets
***
Fruit Salad   Assorted Cookies
Coffee

◆ SPAIN ◆

GAZPACHO
Cold Salad Soup

Preparation Time: 15 minutes   *Serves 4–6*
(*Does not include chilling time.*)

An interesting Spanish soup. This liquid salad of tomatoes, garlic, onion, green pepper and cucumber must be served ice cold.

INGREDIENTS

1 garlic clove
1 small onion, sliced
3 ripe tomatoes, cored, seeded and quartered
½ green pepper, seeded and sliced
1 small cucumber, peeled and sliced
1½ tablespoons red wine vinegar
1½ tablespoons olive oil
¾ cup tomato juice
½ teaspoon salt
⅛ teaspoon cayenne pepper or to taste

TO MAKE CROUTONS

2 tablespoons olive oil
1 cup bread cubes
1 garlic clove, split

DIRECTIONS

Prepare vegetables and place in blender with vinegar, olive oil, tomato juice, salt, and cayenne pepper.
Cover and purée for 4 seconds.
Correct seasoning if necessary. Chill.

Serve with diced cucumber, chopped scallion, chopped green pepper, a finely chopped hard-boiled egg, and croutons. Let each person add the condiments he or she likes.

Croutons can be purchased, but here's how to make them. Heat olive oil in small skillet; add bread cubes and garlic.
Sauté, stirring occasionally, until golden brown. Discard garlic.
Drain croutons on absorbent paper.

ARROZ CON POLLO
Chicken with Rice

Preparation and Baking Time: 1 hour 30 minutes   Serves 4

Chicken baked on a bed of saffron rice is a Spanish dish that has gained tremendous popularity in America.

INGREDIENTS

1 3-pound chicken, cut up
1 teaspoon salt
¼ teaspoon freshly ground black pepper
¼ teaspoon paprika
⅓ cup oil
½ tablespoon lemon juice

1 medium onion, chopped
1 garlic clove, minced

1 cup uncooked rice
⅛ teaspoon saffron
4 cups canned tomatoes, undrained
1 green pepper, cored, seeded, and chopped
1 teaspoon salt

DIRECTIONS

Sprinkle chicken with salt, pepper, and paprika.

Heat oil in large skillet until hot; brown chicken on all sides.

Sprinkle browned chicken with lemon juice.

Remove chicken from pan and arrange in a shallow 3-quart casserole.

Sauté onion and garlic in oil in skillet until limp and golden; sprinkle over top of chicken.

Sprinkle rice and saffron on chicken in the casserole; add tomatoes with green pepper. Season with salt.

Cover tightly and bake at 350° F. for 1 hour.

SPANISH DINNER
Gazpacho

Arroz con Pollo
Escarole
with Oil and Vinegar

Fresh Mangoes
Coffee

◈ ITALY ◈

SPAGHETTI WITH MEAT BALLS

Preparation and Cooking Time: 2 hours 15 minutes   Serves 4

Spaghetti and meat balls or meat sauce is one of the top ten food favorites in this country. This recipe comes from my mother-in-law, Mrs. Frank (Anna) Torre.

INGREDIENTS
3 tablespoons olive oil
2 garlic cloves, halved
1 2-pound 3-ounce can Italian plum tomatoes, undrained
1 teaspoon salt
1 tablespoon minced fresh parsley or 1 teaspoon dried parsley

DIRECTIONS
You can buy tomato sauce in the store or make it yourself. It's best to make it. Heat olive oil in a large sauce pot and sauté garlic until limp; strain tomatoes through food mill into pot or purée tomatoes in blender for a few seconds before adding

½ teaspoon basil
⅛ teaspoon freshly ground black pepper

to pot. Add salt, parsley, basil, and black pepper; simmer 1 hour.

(NOTE: This is the basic tomato sauce used in countless recipes. You can make all sorts of different toppings for spaghetti simply by adding different ingredients such as lobster, clams, shrimp, fried sausage, fried ground beef, peas, mushrooms, tuna fish, and many, many others. Vary the seasoning with a pinch of oregano or crushed red pepper.)

TO MAKE MEAT BALLS

1 pound ground beef
2 slices stale white bread, grated
2 tablespoons freshly grated Romano or Parmesan cheese
1 garlic clove, minced
1 tablespoon minced fresh parsley
⅛ teaspoon freshly grated black pepper
3 medium eggs

Mix together in a large bowl the ground beef, bread crumbs, grated cheese, garlic, parsley, and black pepper.
Add eggs one at a time. Mixture should not be too loose or the meat balls will fall apart when fried. Wet hands in cold water before forming meat mixture into round balls, about 2 inches in diameter. Handle meat mixture gently. *Do not pack meat balls.*

Oil for frying	Heat at least ½ inch of oil in a large skillet. Fry meat balls until crisp and brown on all sides; drain on absorbent paper. Add meat balls to sauce and simmer 1 hour more.
1 pound spaghetti, cooked al dente *and drained* *¼ cup freshly grated Parmesan or Romano cheese*	Remove drained pasta to warmed platter; ladle just enough sauce over the top to coat the pasta lightly. Sprinkle with cheese, toss and serve. Meat balls are usually passed separately. Pass extra cheese and sauce.

VARIATIONS

This sauce waits beautifully for company and can be frozen.

Form tiny meat balls the size of large marbles, fry, and add to sauce.

Serve over hot cooked rice.

ITALIAN GARLIC BREAD

Preparation and Cooking Time: 15 minutes   *Serves 4–6*

So easy and so delicious.

INGREDIENTS
1 loaf Italian bread
Butter, at room temperature
Garlic salt

DIRECTIONS
Preheat oven to 400° F. Cut diagonal slices from a loaf of Italian bread. Spread slices with butter. Sprinkle with garlic salt.
Arrange on baking sheet. Heat about 10 minutes until hot and lightly browned.

ITALIAN DINNER
Antipasto

Spaghetti with Meat Balls
**Mixed Green Salad
with Oil and Vinegar**
Italian Garlic Bread

**Biscuit Tortoni
Espresso**

◈ GREECE ◈

GREEK EGG-LEMON SOUP WITH MEAT BALLS

Preparation and Cooking Time: 45 minutes *Serves 4*

Mrs. Chrysanthe Pampris LaRosa serves this hearty soup as a complete meal with Italian or French bread.

INGREDIENTS

2 quarts canned chicken broth

Salt and freshly ground black pepper to taste

TO MAKE MEAT BALLS

1 pound ground beef

¼ cup uncooked white rice, washed well and drained thoroughly

3 tablespoons minced fresh mint or 1½ tablespoons dried mint

1 teaspoon salt

¼ teaspoon freshly ground black pepper

TO MAKE SAUCE

2 large eggs, well beaten

Juice of a lemon
  or 2 ounces lemon juice

DIRECTIONS

Heat chicken broth while you make the meat balls.
Season to taste.

Mix together in a large bowl the ground beef, rice, mint, salt, and black pepper.
Wet hands in cold water before forming meat mixture into round balls, about the size of a walnut. Handle meat mixture gently. *Do not pack meat balls.*
Add meat balls to hot broth and cook 30 minutes.

When ready to serve, beat eggs in a 4-cup measuring cup (this makes it easy to pour later on) or a large bowl. Add lemon juice.
Slowly stir some of the hot broth into the eggs. Continue to beat while adding more broth until cup is full.
Stir egg-lemon mixture into soup; continue to mix so eggs won't curdle. Remove from heat. Let stand, covered, for 5 minutes, to thicken. Serve at once.

VARIATIONS

Without the meat balls, this is Greek egg-lemon soup. You can also cook manestra (a type of pasta) in broth before adding the egg-lemon mixture.

GREEK SUPPER
*Greek Egg-Lemon Soup
with Meat Balls*
Greek, Italian,
or French Bread

Fresh Fruit   Coffee

◈ JAPAN ◈

TEMPURA

Preparation and Cooking Time: 1 hour   *Serves 3–4*

This classic Japanese dish of fried shrimps and vegetables is dramatic but simple. Freelance artist Carol Inouye stresses that great care is always taken to arrange the food beautifully.

INGREDIENTS

1 pound (*allow 2 or 3 per person*) *large fresh shrimps, shelled and deveined*

DIRECTIONS

Have shrimp cleaned in the fish store or do it yourself. Shell the shrimp, but leave the tail attached. Split each

2 medium potatoes, peeled and sliced ¼ inch thick
1 medium green pepper, cored, seeded and sliced into ¼-inch vertical strips
2 medium carrots, cleaned and cut into ¼-inch vertical strips
20 fresh string beans, washed and stemmed
6 small scallions with green part, cut into 2-inch-long pieces

TO MAKE BATTER
1 large egg
1 cup ice-cold water
¼ teaspoon sugar
⅛ teaspoon baking soda
1 cup flour

Oil for frying

shrimp down the back and remove the black intestinal vein.
Wash in cold water; dry on absorbent paper. Set aside.
All the ingredients must be prepared before you begin to fry. Clean vegetables.
Slice the peeled potatoes into ¼-inch slices.
Slice pepper and carrots into ¼-inch vertical strips.
Leave string beans whole.
Cut scallions into 2-inch-long pieces. Great care should be taken to cut the vegetables evenly.

Beat egg and ice-cold water together in a mixing bowl; add sugar and baking soda. Gradually mix in flour with a whisk or fork. Do not overmix. The batter should be lumpy.

Fill a deep 10- or 12-inch frying pan with 2 inches of oil. Heat oil until hot.

To test, dip one shrimp into the batter and place in the oil. If the oil bubbles, it is hot enough to begin frying.

Dip 6 or 7 shrimps into the batter and place in frying pan with tongs.

Fry until light golden brown, about a minute; turn over and fry other side.

Remove from pan and drain on absorbent paper.

Repeat process until all the shrimps are fried.

Be careful of spattering oil. If oil gets too hot or smoky, lower heat.

Skim particles of fried batter with a mesh skimmer once in a while, as these will burn and discolor the oil.

After the shrimps, fry the potatoes, then the carrots, string beans, pepper, and lastly the scallions. Keep warm in oven.

Soy sauce

To serve arrange 3 shrimp and 2 or 3 pieces of each vegetable on each warmed plate. Serve with soy sauce.

CUCUMBER SALAD

Preparation Time: 35 minutes *Serves 2–3*
(*Does not include chilling time.*)

INGREDIENTS

1 large cucumber, peeled and sliced paper thin

1 tablespoon soy sauce
1 tablespoon vinegar

DIRECTIONS

After peeling and slicing cucumber, sprinkle with salt.
Let stand 30 minutes or until wilted.
Drain and rinse with water.

Add soy sauce and vinegar.
Chill before serving.

JAPANESE DINNER
Tempura
Cucumber Salad

Tangerine Sections
Tea

HOLIDAY DISHES

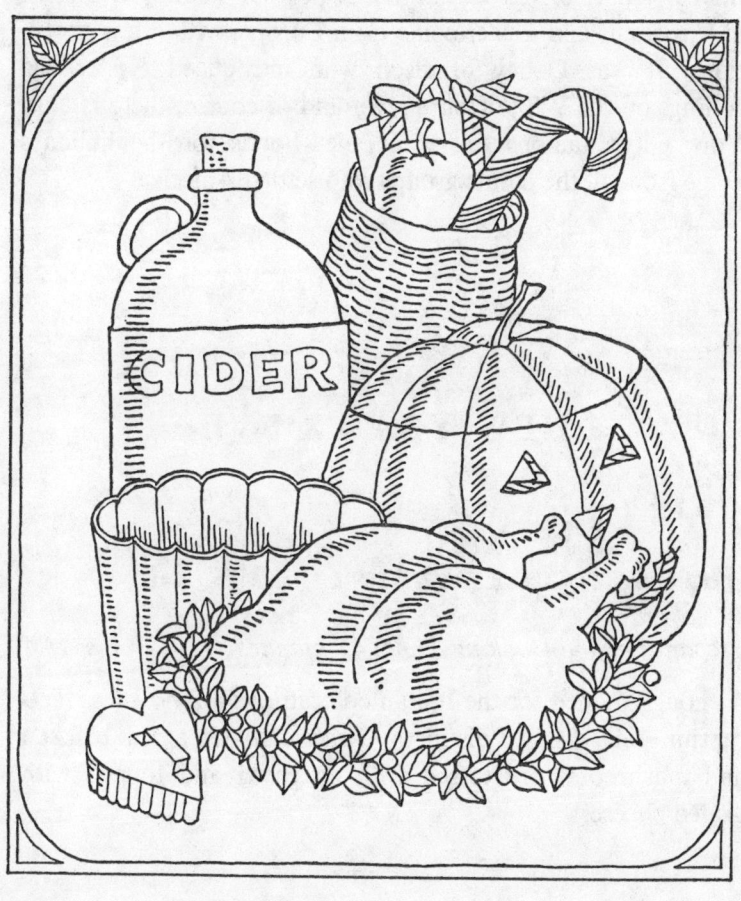

Some holidays are uniquely American. Thanksgiving is probably the most American of holidays. Wild turkey, cranberries, stewed pumpkin, Indian pudding and other corn dishes—all original natives of America—must surely have graced that first Thanksgiving the Pilgrims shared with Massasoit and his tribe. Other historic and patriotic holidays include the Fourth of July, Memorial Day, Lincoln's Birthday, and Washington's Birthday. Memorial Day heralds the beginning of numerous summer picnics. Mother's Day and Father's Day are American inventions. Both became nation-wide occasions during the early part of this century. Most of our holiday traditions at Christmas and Easter come from Europe, with a few exceptions. It was Dolley Madison who introduced Easter egg rollings on the White House lawn and of course, there is New York City's famous Easter parade. Foods for the holidays come from all the ethnic groups who settled America.

◆ NEW YEAR'S EVE ◆

CHICKEN TETRAZZINI

Preparation and Cooking Time: 45 minutes *Serves 4*

Although named for the Italian coloratura soprano Luisa Tetrazzini, this dish is distinctly American. Creamed chicken and mushrooms are tossed with spaghetti and topped with grated cheese.

INGREDIENTS

4 tablespoons butter
4 tablespoons flour
¼ teaspoon nutmeg
1 teaspoon salt
⅛ teaspoon freshly ground black pepper
Pinch of cayenne pepper
2½ cups chicken stock

4 tablespoons butter
½ pound fresh mushrooms, cleaned and sliced
1 teaspoon fresh lemon juice

1½ cups chopped cooked chicken

½ pound package spaghetti, cooked and drained
⅔ cup freshly grated Parmesan or Romano cheese

DIRECTIONS

Blend flour and seasonings in melted butter in a medium saucepan; add chicken stock, and cook, stirring constantly, until thick and smooth.

In a small frying pan, sauté mushrooms in butter until tender, about 5 minutes; add lemon juice and toss together.

Stir mushrooms and chicken into sauce.
Remove from heat.

Toss hot cooked spaghetti, ⅓ cup cheese, and sauce in a shallow casserole; top with remaining cheese.
Brown until bubbly in a preheated 350° F. oven, about 10–15 minutes.

VARIATIONS

This dish can also be served immediately after spaghetti has been tossed with sauce and grated cheese. As a casserole, this dish can be prepared in advance.

NEW YEAR'S EVE BUFFET
Chicken Tetrazzini
Asparagus with Lemon Butter
Cranberry-Orange Relish (page 73)
Rolls   Butter

Chocolate Ice Box Cake (page 117)

===

❖ ST. VALENTINE'S DAY ❖

CHOCOLATE-DIPPED ORANGE PEEL

Preparation and Cooking Time: 30 minutes

Makes about 1 pound

(Does not include cooling or drying time.)

This mid-February holiday has been a festival of romance since the days of ancient Rome when Juno and Pan were feted. After the coming of Christianity, the holiday was named in honor of Bishop Valentine. My husband, Frank, makes me candied orange peel dipped in melted chocolate for a special, inexpensive treat.

INGREDIENTS	DIRECTIONS
6 medium oranges	Strip peel from washed
Cold water to cover	sections.

Put peel in a saucepan with enough cold water to cover.
Bring to a boil; reduce heat and simmer 15 minutes or until soft. Drain peel.
Scrape off white part with a spoon and cut peel in thin strips with kitchen scissors.

2 cups sugar
½ cup water

Put sugar and water in saucepan.
Heat, stirring constantly, until sugar dissolves.
Add orange peel and cook slowly until peel is almost transparent (230° on a candy thermometer) and absorbs some of the syrup.
Watch carefully to avoid burning.
Drain and spread on a plate or wire rack to cool.
(NOTE: At this point you can roll candied peel in granulated sugar. Dry on wax paper before storing in an airtight glass container.)

Melted semisweet or sweet chocolate

Dip candied peel in melted chocolate.
Dry on wax paper until chocolate is hard.
Store in airtight glass container.

VARIATIONS

Grapefruit or lemon peels can be candied, but to reduce the bitter taste you must soak overnight in cold water with 1 tablespoon salt. Drain and cover with cold water; then bring to a boil. Repeat this 3 times. Then cook until peel is soft. Proceed with recipe.

◈ LINCOLN'S BIRTHDAY ◈

GINGERBREAD WITH LEMON SAUCE

Preparation and Baking Time: 1 hour

Makes one 10-inch square cake

Our great Civil War President, Abraham Lincoln, cared little for food, but he did enjoy burnt-sugar cakes, corn cakes, and gingerbread. George Washington's mother served gingerbread to Marquis de La Fayette when he visited Fredericksburg in 1784.

INGREDIENTS

½ *cup shortening*
½ *cup sugar*
1 *large egg, beaten*
1 *cup black molasses*

DIRECTIONS

Preheat oven to 350° F. and grease 10 by 10-inch baking dish. Set aside.
Cream shortening and sugar in a large mixing bowl.

	Add an egg and molasses; beat until smooth.
2½ cups flour 1½ teaspoons baking soda 1 teaspoon cinnamon 1 teaspoon ginger ½ teaspoon ground cloves ½ teaspoon salt	Sift together dry ingredients; add to molasses mixture and beat until smooth.
1 cup hot water	Add hot water last and beat until smooth and well blended. Pour into greased 10-inch baking dish. Bake for 35–40 minutes. Serve with whipped cream or this tangy lemon sauce.

TO MAKE LEMON SAUCE

⅓ cup sugar 1 tablespoon cornstarch 1 cup water	Mix sugar, cornstarch, and water together in a small saucepan. Cook, stirring constantly, until mixture bubbles. Simmer gently until mixture begins to thicken; then remove from heat.
3 tablespoons butter ½ teaspoon grated lemon rind 1½ tablespoons fresh lemon juice Pinch of salt	Stir in butter, lemon rind, lemon juice, and salt. Serve hot over gingerbread.

◆ WASHINGTON'S BIRTHDAY ◆

CHERRY COBBLER

Preparation and Baking Time: 45 minutes

Makes one 8-inch square cake

An old-fashioned treat which seems a fitting choice to serve on George Washington's birthday to remind us of the legend of how he chopped down the cherry tree.

INGREDIENTS

2 cups canned red pitted cherries; drain, reserving juice
1 tablespoon tapioca or flour

⅓ cup sugar
⅛ teaspoon salt
¾ cup cherry juice
½ teaspoon almond extract

¾ cup flour
1 teaspoon baking powder
¼ teaspoon salt
3 tablespoons shortening
6 tablespoons milk
1 medium egg
¼ cup chopped, toasted almonds

DIRECTIONS

Preheat oven to 425° F. and grease 8 by 8-inch baking dish.

Place drained cherries in baking dish.

Sprinkle tapioca or flour over cherries.

Combine sugar, salt, cherry juice, and almond extract; pour over cherries.

Sift flour with baking powder and salt.

Cut in shortening until mixture looks like a fine meal.

Add milk and egg and mix thoroughly.

Stir in almonds until well distributed.

Drop dough by small spoonfuls on cherry mixture and spread slightly.
Bake for 25–30 minutes until lightly browned and bubbly.
Serve hot or cold.
Top with ice cream, sour cream, or whipped cream if you like.

VARIATIONS

Substitute blueberries, peaches, plums, or strawberries. You can also substitute canned fruit or pie filling.

◆ EASTER ◆

CORNISH HENS WITH RICE STUFFING

Preparation and Cooking Time: 2 hours 30 minutes   Serves 4

Diced pork flavors the rice stuffing of this splendid company dish. Mrs. Anthony (Camille) Valeri serves it often on holidays instead of traditional roasts.

INGREDIENTS
1 tablespoon oil
¼ pound pork, diced

DIRECTIONS
Brown pork in oil in a large skillet.
Remove pork from the pan; reserve.

| 1 small onion, finely chopped
1 clove garlic, minced	Sauté onion and garlic in same skillet until limp and golden; remove from pan and reserve with pork.
1 cup uncooked rice
1 tablespoon oil	Add rice and oil to skillet; sauté until rice turns golden. Stir frequently.
2 cups hot chicken broth
Salt and black pepper to taste	Add hot chicken broth, pork, onion, and garlic to rice mixture; cover and simmer 20 minutes or until rice is tender. Season to taste with salt and black pepper.
4 1-pound Cornish hens	Stuff Cornish hens with rice mixture.
Place in greased baking pan; bake, uncovered, at 375° F. for about 1½ hours.
Baste occasionally. |

TO MAKE GRAVY

| 1½ cups chicken broth
⅛ cup sherry
1 cup canned mushrooms	Add to juices from Cornish hens the chicken broth, sherry, and mushrooms; simmer 15 minutes.
1 tablespoon cornstarch
Salt and black pepper to taste	Stir cornstarch into a little of mixture separately; then add to pan, stirring constantly, over low heat until thickened.
Season to taste and serve separately with Cornish hens.

WALDORF SALAD

Preparation Time: 5 minutes　　　　　　　　　Serves 4
(*Does not include chilling time.*)

Created at the Waldorf Astoria Hotel in New York City. It is especially good with pork, ham, or roast chicken.

INGREDIENTS

2 cups diced tart apples
2 tablespoons lemon juice
1 stalk celery, chopped fine
½ cup chopped walnuts
1 cup seedless grapes

½ cup mayonnaise
Salt to taste

DIRECTIONS

Sprinkle apples with lemon juice to keep them from turning dark.
Combine apples with celery, walnuts, and grapes.

Add mayonnaise to apple mixture; toss.
Season to taste with salt.
Chill thoroughly. Serve on crisp lettuce.

EASTER DINNER
French Onion Soup

***Cornish Hens
with Rice Stuffing***
Buttered Green Beans
Waldorf Salad
Cranberry-Orange Relish (page 73)
Rolls　　Butter

Trifle (page 114)
Coffee

◈ ST. PATRICK'S DAY ◈

IRISH SODA BREAD

Preparation and Baking Time: 1 hour 15 minutes
Makes one 9-inch round loaf

Nothing is more Irish than Mrs. Tom (Anne) Conroy's soda bread for breakfast or tea on St. Patrick's Day.

INGREDIENTS

3½ cups sifted flour
3½ teaspoons baking powder
½ teaspoon baking soda
1 teaspoon salt
3 tablespoons sugar

2 tablespoons shortening
1 large egg, beaten lightly
2 cups buttermilk

2 teaspoons caraway seeds
1 cup raisins

DIRECTIONS

Sift together the flour, baking powder, baking soda, salt, and sugar in a large bowl; make a well in the center.

Rub in shortening until mixture is crumbly.
Add egg and buttermilk; mix gently.
Add caraway seeds and raisins, stir lightly and quickly with a wooden spoon into a soft dough.
With floured hands put dough onto a lightly floured board and form dough into a circle.
Place dough on a greased baking sheet or pie tin.

Make a large cross on the top with a floured knife. (This is to ensure even distribution of heat.)
Bake 1 hour in a 400° F. oven or until golden brown.
Test center with a skewer before removing from the oven.
The bread should not be cut until it is quite cold, at least 4 hours old.
To keep bread soft, it is wrapped in a tea towel.

(NOTE: For St. Patrick's Day dinner serve Corned Beef and Cabbage with apple pie and Irish coffee for dessert.)

◈ MOTHER'S DAY ◈

CHICKEN CORDON BLEU

Preparation and Cooking Time: 1 hour   *Serves 4*

Chicken cutlets are substituted in this elegant dish, which is usually made with veal. The result will please everyone—even the cook, because it's easy.

INGREDIENTS

8 medium chicken cutlets (halves of boned and flattened chicken breasts)

8 thin slices of ham
8 slices of Swiss cheese

1 teaspoon salt
¼ cup freshly grated Parmesan cheese
¼ cup flour
1 large egg, beaten
1 tablespoon cold water

4 tablespoons olive oil or butter or a combination

⅛ cup sherry
1 cup chicken broth
1 cup water

⅛ teaspoon garlic salt
⅛ teaspoon celery salt
Pinch of onion flakes
Pinch of freshly ground black pepper

DIRECTIONS

Place cutlets between two pieces of wax paper and pound until as thin as possible. Be careful not to make holes in the cutlet.

Put a slice of ham and cheese on top of each chicken cutlet; roll up and secure with a toothpick.

Sprinkle chicken rolls with salt; roll in mixture of cheese and flour.

Mix egg and water together; dip chicken rolls into mixture.

Let stand 20 minutes.

Heat oil in a large skillet and sauté chicken until brown on all sides.

Remove chicken from pan. Reserve pan drippings.

Pour off excess fat in skillet, leaving ⅓ cup; add sherry, chicken broth, and water; bring to a boil. Lower heat.

Season with garlic salt, celery salt, onion flakes, and black pepper; add mushrooms with liquid and stir.

Simmer over low heat 10

1 3-ounce can mushrooms, undrained

minutes until liquid thickens, stirring occasionally.
Return chicken to skillet and simmer 10 minutes more or until chicken is tender.

MOTHER'S DAY DINNER
Chicken Cordon Bleu
Wild Rice
Peas and Mushrooms
Rolls   Butter
———
Boston Cream Pie (page 115)

═══════════════════════════════

◆ FATHER'S DAY ◆

SHISH KEBAB

Preparation and Cooking Time: 30 minutes   *Serves 4*
(Does not include marinating time.)

A Near Eastern dish of meat, usually lamb, broiled on skewers. The name comes from the Turkish, *shish,* meaning skewer, and *kebab,* meaning roast meat.

INGREDIENTS

2 pounds leg of lamb, cut into 1½-inch cubes
½ cup olive oil
Juice of a large lemon
Salt and black pepper to taste
2 tablespoons minced fresh parsley

SUGGESTED VEGETABLES

Small whole cherry tomatoes or small tomatoes, quartered
Onions, sliced
Green peppers or sweet red peppers, cut into 1½-inch pieces
Small whole mushrooms
Zucchini, sliced

DIRECTIONS

Have a butcher cut lamb into 1½-inch cubes. Marinate at least 2 hours in a mixture of olive oil, lemon juice, salt, black pepper, and parsley.

There is no limit to the variety of shish kebab you can make. Use whatever vegetables are available.

Different foods can be alternated on one skewer or each type strung on a *separate* skewer.

When barbecuing meats and vegetables together, use smaller pieces of meat than vegetables so everything will be done at the same time.

When stringing meat and/or vegetables on skewers, push close together if you want meat rare and juicy; leave space between if you want it crispy and well done.

Broil meat approximately 10 minutes on each side, depending upon your taste. Brush occasionally with marinade.

When barbecuing, a very hot fire is best.

Place about 3 inches above coals for best results. Rotate skewers to cook evenly.

And don't forget to brush with marinade.

VARIATIONS

Beef can be used instead of lamb.

Try wrapping beef with bacon.

FATHER'S DAY BARBECUE
Lamb Shish Kebab
Corn on the Cob
Cole Slaw   Pickles

Chocolate Ice Box Cake (page 117)

◆ FOURTH OF JULY ◆

POTATO SALAD

Preparation and Cooking Time: 30 minutes   *Serves 4–6*
(Does not include chilling time.)

The white potato originated in Peru and was brought to this country by the Spaniards. At first it was thought suitable only for chickens and pigs, and was accepted in England and Ireland in the sixteenth century long before it became popular in the American colonies.

INGREDIENTS

6 medium potatoes, peeled, cubed, and cooked
3 hard-boiled eggs, coarsely chopped

1 cup chopped onion
1 cup sliced celery
2 tablespoons chopped fresh parsley

½ cup vegetable oil
¼ cup tarragon vinegar
2 teaspoons salt
1 teaspoon sugar
¼ teaspoon paprika

¾ cup mayonnaise

DIRECTIONS

Cook potatoes in rapidly simmering water until tender. Drain and cool slightly.
Cook eggs at the same time. Remove shells and chop coarsely.

Mix potatoes and chopped eggs with onion, celery, and parsley.

Blend together in a small bowl the oil, vinegar, salt, sugar and paprika; pour over potato mixture.
Cover and refrigerate at least 2 hours.

Just before serving, toss with mayonnaise.

DEVILED EGGS

Preparation and Cooking Time: 15 minutes   Makes 12
(*Does not include time to boil eggs or to chill.*)

A perennial favorite at picnics.

INGREDIENTS
6 hard-boiled eggs

¼ cup mayonnaise
¼ teaspoon salt
⅛ teaspoon freshly ground black pepper
½ teaspoon mustard
2 teaspoons minced onion
6 stuffed green olives, sliced in half

DIRECTIONS
Slice cooled eggs in half lengthwise.
Scoop yolks out and mash in small bowl.
Reserve whites.

Mix the remaining ingredients together except the olive slices; combine with the mashed egg yolks.
Fill whites with yolk mixture.
Garnish with olive half. Chill.

FOURTH OF JULY PICNIC
Deviled Eggs
Cold Fried Chicken
Potato Salad
Bean Salad
Carrots and Cucumber Sticks

Brownies (page 104)
Watermelon

◆ HALLOWEEN ◆

POPCORN BALLS

Preparation and Cooking Time: 30 minutes   Makes 2½ dozen

American Indians introduced early colonists to corn that popped over heat. Popcorn balls make ideal party food.

INGREDIENTS

3 quarts freshly popped corn
½ teaspoon salt

1 cup light molasses
1 cup white corn syrup
1 tablespoon vinegar

3 tablespoons butter

DIRECTIONS

Put popped corn in a large bowl and sprinkle with salt. Set aside.

Mix the molasses, syrup, and vinegar in a heavy saucepan.

Cook over medium heat until a little syrup dropped into a cup of cold water separates into threads which are hard but not brittle, or a candy thermometer reads 270° F.

Remove from the heat; add the butter and stir briefly to mix.

Pour the syrup over the popcorn and stir constantly to coat it evenly.

When it is cool enough to handle, butter your hands and form popcorn into 2-inch balls.

Let cool on wax paper.

When cooled, wrap each ball in wax paper; then in colored cellophane.

VARIATIONS

Substitute 2 cups white corn syrup or use 1 cup molasses with 1 cup sugar. Proceed as directed in recipe.

Add 2 cups chopped cashews or ½ cup chopped candied red or green cherries.

Hang on the Christmas tree as a decoration.

HOT SPICED APPLE CIDER

Preparation and Cooking Time: 15 minutes   *Serves 6*

Here's a recipe for a Colonial punch that's perfect for a brisk fall day.

INGREDIENTS

1 quart apple cider
3 cinnamon sticks
4 tablespoons fresh lemon juice

1 teaspoon nutmeg
1 teaspoon whole cloves

DIRECTIONS

Simmer cider, cinnamon sticks, and lemon juice for 15 minutes in a large saucepan.

Tie nutmeg and cloves in a small cheesecloth bag; put into the simmering cider just long enough to give it the desired taste. Remove and serve hot.

HALLOWEEN PARTY
Popcorn Balls
Gingerbread
with Lemon Sauce (page 54)
Hot Spiced Apple Cider

❖ THANKSGIVING ❖

ROAST TURKEY

Preparation and Cooking Time: 4 hours Serves 8–10
(*Time depends on size of turkey used.*)

Americans rarely think of turkey—an original native of America—without thinking of the first Thanksgiving which the Pilgrims shared with Massasoit and his tribe.

INGREDIENTS

1 8–10 pound turkey

TO MAKE STUFFING

¼ pound sausage
½ cup diced onion
½ cup diced celery

3 cups fresh bread crumbs
3 cups corn bread crumbs
1 cup diced apple,
  or 1 cup chopped dried apricots or prunes

DIRECTIONS

Wash and set aside to drain.

Fry sausage in a large skillet until almost done. Add onion and celery; cook until the onion is limp and golden. Remove from heat.

Add bread crumbs, corn bread crumbs, diced apple, raisins, salt, black pepper, eggs, and chicken broth to skillet; mix together thoroughly with

¼ cup raisins
2 teaspoons salt
⅛ teaspoon freshly ground black pepper
2 large eggs, beaten
¼ cup chicken broth

2 tablespoons butter, at room temperature
4 slices of bacon or salt pork

sausage mixture. Stuffing should not be too loose.
Stuff wishbone cavity lightly and skewer or sew skin to back.
Shape the wings akimbo, bringing tips onto back of wings.
Fill the body cavity with stuffing.
Do not pack it, as it expands when cooked.
To close the cavity, place skewers across it and lace it closed with cord.
Tie drumsticks securely to the tail or place through a slit made in the skin.
Place stuffed turkey, breast side up, on a rack in an open roasting pan.
Grease turkey surface well with butter.
Place slices of bacon over the breast.
Roast in a moderate 375° F. oven.
Baste every 30 minutes with fat from pan.
If breast of turkey begins to brown too quickly, cover with foil.
Allow 20–25 minutes per pound.

To test for doneness, move the leg joint up and down; it should give readily.
Or pierce the thigh; if the juice that runs out is clear with no tinge of pink, the bird is done. When the turkey is quite tender, take from oven; place on a large heated serving dish; return to warm oven to keep hot.
Pour off most of fat in pan.
Add a little water to pan juices, stirring and scraping sides of the pan, and cook on top of the stove for 5 minutes.
Serve turkey with pan juices.
Stuffing is removed whole, if possible, and sliced.

VARIATIONS

This stuffing is delicious baked in a buttered baking dish separately.
Top with bacon slices or dots of butter.
Excellent with pork.
Or top stuffing with chicken pieces and bake covered at 350° F. for 1 hour or until the chicken is tender and golden.

CRANBERRY-ORANGE RELISH

Preparation Time: 5 minutes   *Serves 4*
(Does not include marinating time.)

Cranberries may first have been known as "crane berries," since cranes living in New England bogs ate the berries. First associated with Massachusetts they were also known as "bounce berries," since they were tested for ripeness by bouncing them.

INGREDIENTS	DIRECTIONS
1 medium unpeeled, seedless orange 2 cups raw cranberries, washed	Put the orange and cranberries through a food chopper.
1 cup sugar	Mix with the sugar and allow to stand overnight in a covered container in the refrigerator.

THANKSGIVING DINNER
Fresh Fruit Cup

Roast Turkey
with Sausage-Corn Bread Stuffing
Creamed Onions
or Baked Butternut Squash
Candied Sweet Potatoes
Waldorf Salad (page 59)
Cranberry-Orange Relish
Rolls   **Butter**

Pumpkin Pie (page 110)   **Indian Pudding (page 98)**
Coffee

◈ CHRISTMAS ◈

FRUITCAKE

Preparation and Baking Time: 2 hours
　　　　　Makes one large 10- or 12-inch fruit cake
(Does not include cooling time. Keep fruitcake at least a week before eating.)

Fruitcake was *the* cake in Colonial times. It is still very popular all year round for any festive occasion. This is the fruitcake Mrs. Jimmy (Louise) Palazzo serves every Christmas.

INGREDIENTS
2 cups water
2 cups sugar
¼ pound plus ⅛ pound butter
½ box dark raisins

1 teaspoon vanilla
1 tablespoon plus 1 teaspoon rum

3 cups flour
1 teaspoon baking powder
1 teaspoon baking soda
¼ teaspoon salt
¼ teaspoon cinnamon
¼ teaspoon ground cloves
¼ teaspoon allspice

2 large eggs, beaten
1 small carton diced fruits
1 cup chopped walnuts

DIRECTIONS
Put water, sugar, butter, and raisins in a saucepan; heat to boiling point.
Boil gently 5 minutes.
Remove from heat.

Add vanilla and rum; mix thoroughly.
Cool for 1–1½ hours.

Sift together flour, baking powder, baking soda, salt, cinnamon, cloves, and allspice into large mixing bowl.

Beat eggs; add eggs and raisin mixture to flour mixture. Mix thoroughly.
Add diced fruits (cut cherries

	in half or leave whole) and walnuts to batter.
	Mix together thoroughly.
	Pour batter into large buttered and floured, 10- or 12-inch spring tube pan.
	Bake at 375° F. for 30 minutes; reduce heat to 350° F. and bake 1 hour more.
Rum to taste	Cool fruitcake in pan. Sprinkle rum on cloth to keep moist. Wrap in foil, Saran Wrap, or wax paper, and store in an airtight tin.
	Keep in a cool place.
	Keep fruitcake at least a week before eating. Flavors will blend and become mellow with age. Fruitcake slices better if chilled.

EGGNOG

Preparation and Cooking Time: 15 minutes   *Serves 6–8*
(Does not include chilling time.)

Eggnog is an American drink with English ancestors. It is one of the traditional drinks served at Christmastime, especially in our southern states.

INGREDIENTS	DIRECTIONS
3 large eggs, at room temperature	Separate eggs. Reserve egg whites.

⅓ cup sugar ¼ teaspoon salt	Beat sugar into egg yolks until lemony in color. Add salt.
4 cups milk, scalded	Heat milk until scalded. Stir milk into egg mixture very slowly. Cook in the top of a double boiler over hot, not boiling water, stirring constantly, until mixture coats spoon (about 1 minute). Cool.
3 tablespoons sugar 1 teaspoon vanilla or 2 tablespoons sherry	Beat reserved egg whites until foamy. Gradually add sugar, beating until soft peaks form. Add vanilla and meringue to custard; mix thoroughly. Chill 4 hours. Pour into punch bowl.
1 cup heavy cream, whipped 1 tablespoon sugar Nutmeg	Beat sugar with heavy cream; drop by tablespoonfuls onto top of eggnog. Sprinkle with nutmeg. Serve at once.

CHRISTMAS CAROLERS' SNACK
Fruitcake
Coconut-Butter Cookies (page 103)
Eggnog

LUNCH AND SUPPER DISHES

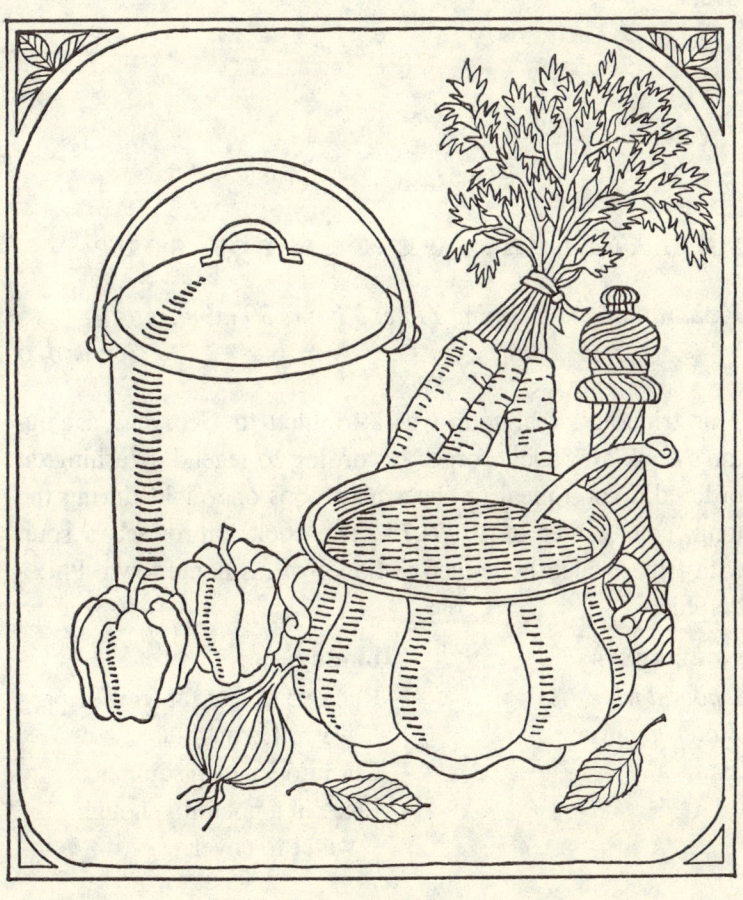

Americans on the go have always favored meals for lunch or supper that can be prepared quickly or possibly be prepared ahead of time. Soup has become the mainstay of a light meal at home. Soup and a sandwich, soup and a salad, or soup and fruit—all are popular choices. Homemade soups are fun to make and once in the pot require little watching. Americans have always consumed enormous amounts of hamburgers and hot dogs, and now pizza joins these in popularity. Made in advance, it can be popped into the oven on a moment's notice. Casseroles and salads offer an excellent way to use up leftovers.

PHILADELPHIA PEPPER POT SOUP

Preparation and Cooking Time: 3 hours 30 minutes

Serves 4–6

This tripe and veal soup was attributed to George Washington's cook at Valley Forge. According to legend, Washington ordered a good meal to cheer his troops one night during the long, cold winter of 1777–78. The cook improvised a soup with tripe, which he named in honor of his home town, Philadelphia.

INGREDIENTS
1 pound tripe
Water to cover

DIRECTIONS
Remove excess fat from tripe; wash thoroughly.
Cut into ½-inch squares.
Place in a pot with enough water to cover.

	Bring to a boil; lower heat and simmer tripe gently for 10 minutes to remove excess fat.
	(Simmering *without* boiling is the secret of making tripe tender.)
	Drain. Set aside.
1 veal shank, cut into 3 parts	Place veal in large enamel soup pot with water.
2 quarts water	Add drained tripe, bay leaf, onions, salt, and black pepper.
1 bay leaf	
3 medium onions, sliced thin	
1 tablespoon salt	Simmer 1 hour.
¼ teaspoon freshly ground black pepper or peppercorns	
2 stalks celery with leaves, chopped	Add celery, carrots, tomatoes, green pepper, parsley, cloves, and thyme; cook at a simmer 1 hour longer.
3 carrots, diced	
2 cups canned tomatoes, undrained	
1 medium green pepper, seeded and diced	
3 tablespoons chopped fresh parsley	
3 whole cloves	
½ teaspoon thyme	
3 medium potatoes peeled and diced	Add potatoes and simmer 1 hour longer or until tripe is tender and veal is falling off the bone.

Remove bone and take off meat.
Cut into small pieces; return meat to soup.
Correct seasoning if necessary.
Remove peppercorns, cloves, and bay leaf before serving.
This soup keeps well and can be reheated.
In fact, tripe tastes better the second time.

U. S. SENATE BEAN SOUP

Preparation and Cooking Time: 2 hours 30 minutes

Serves 6–8

Save the bone from a baked ham to make this hearty soup. The addition of mashed potatoes is the secret of this famous soup served in the Senate restaurant. Harry S Truman liked it.

INGREDIENTS

1 pound (2 cups) *dried white beans, washed and drained*

1 *leftover ham bone with meat or 1 large smoked ham hock*

3 *quarts water*

½ *cup cooked mashed potatoes*

DIRECTIONS

Place beans, ham bone and water in large enamel soup pot.

Bring to a boil for 10 minutes; then lower heat and simmer rapidly for 1 hour. (Beans are cooked uncovered because when covered they tend to split.)

Add mashed potatoes, onions, celery, garlic, and parsley;

3 medium onions, chopped
    fine
6 celery stalks with tops,
    chopped fine
1 garlic clove, minced
¼ cup finely chopped fresh
    parsley

Salt and black pepper to
    taste

add more water if necessary;
simmer 1 hour or until
beans are tender.

Remove ham bone from soup;
cut up pieces of meat;
return ham to soup.

Season with salt and pepper to
taste.

SPLIT PEA SOUP

Preparation and Cooking Time: 2 hours 15 minutes   Serves 4

Since the early days of the fur trade when it was introduced by the French-Canadians, this soup has been a favorite in the Northwest.

INGREDIENTS

¼ pound salt pork, diced

DIRECTIONS

Brown salt pork in medium
    soup pot.
Remove crisp salt pork bits;
    reserve.

1 medium onion, chopped
1 garlic clove, minced
1 stalk celery with leaves,
    chopped

Cook onion, garlic, and celery
in fat until the onion is limp
and golden.

1 cup green split peas
1 quart water
1 teaspoon salt
¼ teaspoon freshly ground
    black pepper
1 bay leaf

Add peas, water, salt, black
pepper, and bay leaf. Bring
to a boil; lower heat and
simmer covered about 2
hours.
Correct seasoning if necessary.

Remove bay leaf.
Sprinkle with reserved pork bits before serving.

VARIATIONS

Use a ham bone or hock instead of salt pork. Put all of the ingredients in pot together at one time and cook for 2 hours.

CHICKEN-CORN CHOWDER

Preparation and Cooking Time: 30 minutes *Serves 4*

A favorite in Lancaster County, Pennsylvania, where it is often served on picnics during the summer.

INGREDIENTS	DIRECTIONS
2 cups cream-style corn 1½ cups chicken broth or water	Bring corn and chicken broth to a boil in a medium soup pot; reduce heat and simmer gently 20 minutes.

1 tablespoon butter
    or margarine
3 tablespoons chopped
    green pepper
1 tablespoon chopped onion
	Sauté green pepper and onion until limp in a small skillet. Remove pan from heat.

2 teaspoons flour 1 teaspoon salt ⅛ teaspoon freshly ground black pepper ¼ cup milk	Blend in flour, salt, and black pepper until smooth; gradually add milk, stirring constantly, until thick and smooth.

2 cups chopped cooked chicken	Stir into corn mixture; bring to a boil; reduce heat.
	Add chicken and milk; stir until blended and hot.
1¾ cups milk	Adjust seasoning if necessary.

PEANUT BUTTER HAMBURGERS

Preparation and Cooking Time: 15 minutes Serves 4

My peanut-butter-loving nephews, Christopher and Nicholas, love this protein-filled discovery of their mother, Mrs. Vincent (Rosemary) Torre. The name for the hamburger sandwich comes from Hamburg, Germany, but it was the Americans who placed the meat in a bun and created what is now considered an American specialty.

INGREDIENTS	DIRECTIONS
¼ cup peanut butter	Mix peanut butter and ground beef until thoroughly blended.
1 pound ground beef	Shape into four large hamburger patties at least ½ inch thick.
	Cook hamburgers in a hot greased skillet or pan broil on a sizzling hot griddle.
	If broiled in an oven, place 3 inches from the heat. Allow 8–12 minutes, turning the hamburgers once.
	If cooked in a skillet or pan-broiled, allow 4 to 8

	minutes for a thick hamburger, turning once. If thin, allow 2 to 6 minutes, turning once.
	Don't flatten or "spank" patties with spatula as it presses out juices.
4 warmed hamburger buns	When done to taste, place in warmed hamburger buns and serve while hot.

VARIATIONS

Here's the best and the easiest recipe I've ever found to stretch a little hamburger to feed a crowd.

Mix the available hamburger with plenty of catsup until it oozes.

Split hamburger buns or English muffins in half (or use slices of white bread), top each half with the hamburger-catsup mixture. Stretch it to make enough for everybody.

Bake in a preheated 400° F. oven 10 minutes or until browned and bubbly. Serve hot.

CLASSY HOT DOGS

Preparation and Cooking Time: 20 minutes *Serves 4–6*

Hot dogs reputedly came to America from Frankfurt, Germany. They became known as "hot dogs" when a cartoonist characterized the "red hot" as an elongated bun containing a dachshund. Much has been made of the fact that the Franklin Roosevelts served hot dogs to the King and Queen of England when they visited.

INGREDIENTS

1 can refrigerated crescent rolls
2 tablespoons mustard
8 frankfurters

DIRECTIONS

Spread mustard on one side of crescent dough.
Place frankfurter on wide end of crescent dough; roll up.
Place on a greased cookie sheet; bake in a preheated 375° F. oven 12–14 minutes or until golden brown.
Serve hot.

PIZZA

Preparation and Cooking Time: 2 hours 30 minutes
Makes three 14-inch pizzas

Since World War II this Italian favorite has gained tremendous popularity. In Italian the word *pizza* means "pie." Prepared in advance, pizza makes fine party fare.

INGREDIENTS
TO MAKE DOUGH

DIRECTIONS

Dough may now be purchased frozen in many supermarkets or fresh at stores selling pizza, but here's how to make the dough if you'd like to.

1 package dry yeast 1 cup lukewarm water	Dissolve yeast in lukewarm water (110° to 115°). Let it stand for 2–3 minutes, then stir yeast into the water until completely dissolved. If yeast does not bubble, start over again with fresh yeast. Set aside.
4 cups flour Pinch of salt	Sift flour and salt in mound on pastry board; make a well in center of flour; pour yeast mixture into well.

Mix dough with fingers or fork.

When you can gather it into a rough ball, place dough on floured board and knead it for 10 minutes or until smooth and elastic.

Add more flour if dough is too wet, or wet your hands in water if too dry.

Place in large greased bowl; cover with plate; set in warm, draft-free spot (oven with heat turned off is ideal) for 1½ hours or until dough has doubled in bulk.

(While dough is rising, prepare sauce.)

When dough has risen, punch down and knead dough lightly for a minute.

Then divide into 3 parts; place each dough ball on a well-oiled pizza pan.

Push the dough evenly with fingers until it is stretched to cover the bottom of pan. Dough should not be thicker than ¼ inch.

TO MAKE SAUCE

You can buy canned sauce in the supermarket, but here's how to make your own if you'd like to.

1 2-pound 3-ounce can Italian plum tomatoes, undrained

Blend briefly in the electric blender or crush tomatoes by squeezing gently with fingers of one hand if you like a lumpy tomato sauce. Set aside.

3 tablespoons olive oil
1 garlic clove, minced
1 teaspoon salt
½ teaspoon basil
⅛ teaspoon freshly ground black pepper

Sauté garlic in olive oil in a medium saucepan until limp.

Add tomatoes, salt, basil, and black pepper.

Cook 20 minutes.

2 tablespoons olive oil
1 8-ounce mozzarella, sliced or grated into tiny strips
½ cup freshly grated Romano or Parmesan cheese

To make pizzas, spread top of pizza dough with olive oil; then top with tomato sauce. Sprinkle with mozzarella and grated cheese.

(At this point pizzas may be frozen.)

Bake at 475° F. for 15–20 minutes until bottom of pizza is golden brown and top bubbly. Cut into wedges and serve at once.

VARIATIONS

Add sliced dried or cooked sausage, sliced mushrooms, fresh minced green pepper, anchovy, or oregano.

Instead of topping pizza dough with tomato sauce, spread with olive oil, then minced garlic.

For "quick" pizza, use an 8-ounce package of refrigerated biscuits.

Flatten each biscuit in a 3-inch round and place on a lightly oiled cookie sheet.

Brush tops with olive oil.

Spread each with about 1½ teaspoons tomato sauce; top with sliced pepperoni and sprinkle with diced mozzarella and grated cheese.

Bake in preheated 400° F. oven 10 minutes or until browned. Makes 10.

Or split English muffins and use with the same topping.

CHOPPED LIVER

Preparation and Cooking Time: 45 minutes
Serves 6–8 as an appetizer

This is as good as you will find in any Jewish delicatessen. The secret of Mrs. Mel (Evie) Sendrovitz's chopped liver is to broil the liver and to use chicken fat.

INGREDIENTS

4 hard-boiled eggs
1 pound chicken livers

2 large onions, diced fine
3 tablespoons chicken fat or vegetable oil

1 tablespoon salt

DIRECTIONS

While eggs are cooking, place chicken livers in a single layer on a rack in a shallow baking pan.

Broil on lowest shelf of the oven for about 10 minutes on each side.

Remove and set aside to cool.

When cool, grind or chop chicken livers quite fine. Set aside.

Grind or mince hard-boiled eggs too.

Reserve.

Heat chicken fat, and sauté onions until limp and golden.

Mix onions, eggs, liver, and salt together gently with a fork.

Correct seasoning if necessary.

If not moist enough, add more chicken fat.

Don't make it like a paste.

Chopped liver should not stick to your mouth like peanut butter.

Serve with crackers and tiny breads or make a sandwich on rye.

PORK CHOW MEIN

Preparation and Cooking Time: 45 minutes   *Serves 4*

An excellent way of using up leftovers. The only difference between chop suey and chow mein is that chow mein is served over crisp Chinese noodles. Both are inventions of Chinese-Americans in San Francisco in the nineteenth century.

INGREDIENTS

¼ cup oil
1 teaspoon salt
¼ teaspoon freshly ground black pepper

2 cups Chinese cabbage, sliced thin
3 cups celery, sliced thin
1 16-ounce can bean sprouts, drained
1 8-ounce can water chestnuts, sliced
2 teaspoons sugar

2 cups chicken broth

DIRECTIONS

Prepare all ingredients before beginning to cook.

Heat oil sprinkled with salt and pepper in a deep, heavy skillet until almost smoking.

Add Chinese cabbage, celery, bean sprouts, water chestnuts, and sugar all at once.

Fry, stirring constantly, for 2 minutes.

Add chicken broth, and cook about 10 minutes.

	Stir occasionally.
2½ tablespoons cornstarch ¼ cup water ¼ cup soy sauce	Mix cornstarch, water, and soy sauce together; add to vegetable mixture. Stir until mixture thickens.
2 cups sliced cooked pork (*thin slivers*)	Add meat and heat thoroughly.
Chow mein noodles, heated	Serve over hot chow mein noodles.

PORK FRIED RICE

Preparation and Cooking Time: 30 minutes   Serves 4

This is probably the most popular Chinese dish in this country, and an excellent way of using up leftovers. All ingredients *must* be prepared before beginning to cook Chinese dishes.

INGREDIENTS	DIRECTIONS
2 tablespoons oil	Heat oil in large skillet.
½ small onion, diced 1 garlic clove, minced 1 teaspoon salt	Add onion and garlic; sprinkle with salt, and cook, stirring occasionally, until limp and golden.
⅓ cup sliced fresh mushrooms ½ cup sliced water chestnuts ⅓ cup frozen peas, thawed and drained	When skillet is sizzling hot, stir fry mushrooms, chestnuts and peas for 2 minutes. (NOTE: "Stir fry" means fry quickly in hot oil while stirring constantly.)

4 cups cooked chilled rice	Add rice and stir fry for 2 minutes more until hot and well mixed with vegetables.
½ cup shredded cooked pork *⅛ teaspoon freshly ground black pepper* *½ teaspoon sugar*	Toss pork, black pepper, and sugar together with rice mixture.
2 tablespoons soy sauce	Add soy sauce to skillet; stir fry for 3 minutes.
1 tablespoon oil *2 eggs, beaten*	Move rice to one side of pan; add oil and then beaten eggs. Allow eggs to begin to set before blending with rice mixture.
1 scallion with green top, chopped fine	Add chopped scallion and stir for 1 minute more. Serve at once.

VARIATIONS

Substitute cooked shrimp or chicken for pork.

TUNA FISH CASSEROLE

Preparation and Cooking Time: 45 minutes   *Serves 4*

A simple dish but very popular. One of the best sporting fish, the tuna belongs to the mackerel family and is caught in the warm-water areas off America, Asia, and Africa. Tuna can be enormous, weighing up to 1,500 pounds.

INGREDIENTS

½ pound green or spinach noodles, cooked al dente and drained

2 tablespoons butter
½ pound sliced fresh mushrooms

1 7-ounce can tuna fish, drained and flaked
½ cup pimiento strips

2 medium eggs
½ cup milk
½ teaspoon salt
½ teaspoon garlic salt
⅛ teaspoon freshly ground black pepper

¼ cup freshly grated Parmesan or Romano cheese
½ cup melted butter

DIRECTIONS

While noodles are cooking, prepare rest of ingredients.

Sauté mushrooms in butter in a small frying pan.

Mix cooked mushrooms with tuna fish and pimiento.

Beat eggs for about half a minute; combine with milk and seasonings.
Add to tuna mixture and cooked, drained noodles.

Sprinkle with grated cheese and dribble melted butter over top.
Bake at 350° F. for 20–25 minutes, or until browned and bubbly.

NEAPOLITAN CASSEROLE

Preparation and Cooking Time: 45 minutes   *Serves 4*

Leftover chicken, tomatoes, and grated cheese are tossed with hot spaghetti, topped with bread crumbs, and baked until brown and bubbly.

INGREDIENTS

4 tablespoons butter
1 medium onion, minced
2 garlic cloves, minced
1 cup sliced fresh mushrooms or 1 cup canned mushrooms, drained

4 tablespoons flour
1½ teaspoons salt
⅛ teaspoon freshly ground black pepper
2 cups chicken stock

2 cups diced cooked chicken
2¼ cups canned tomatoes, undrained
1 cup freshly grated Romano or Parmesan cheese
¼ teaspoon oregano or thyme

1 8-ounce package spaghetti, cooked and drained
½ cup buttered bread crumbs

DIRECTIONS

Sauté in butter in a large saucepan the onion, garlic, and mushrooms until onion is limp and golden.
(NOTE: If canned mushrooms are used, add them with the chicken.)

Blend in flour, salt, and pepper; add stock, and cook, stirring constantly, until stock thickens.

Mix in chicken, tomatoes, cheese, and oregano or thyme.
Remove from heat.

Toss hot, drained spaghetti with chicken-tomato mixture; pour into shallow baking dish; top with bread crumbs. Bake in a preheated 375° F. oven until brown and bubbly, about 15 minutes.

BEST EVER CHICKEN SALAD

Preparation Time: 10 minutes Serves 4
(*Does not include time to cook chicken or to chill.*)

A salad can be a meal in itself. High on the list of favorites is chicken salad served on crisp lettuce. Ingredients should be chilled.

INGREDIENTS

½ cup mayonnaise
¼ cup cider vinegar
3 cups cubed cooked chicken
1½ cups chopped celery
¼ teaspoon capers, drained
Salt and black pepper to taste

2 tablespoons mayonnaise

Lettuce
¼ cup coarsely chopped walnuts
¼ cup golden raisins

DIRECTIONS

Blend mayonnaise with vinegar; combine with chicken, celery, and capers; season with salt and black pepper to taste.

Put salad in bowl and spread surface with mayonnaise. Chill.

Unmold on crisp lettuce and sprinkle with walnuts and raisins.

VARIATIONS

Make up your *own* salad: Cubed pineapple, grapefruit, seedless grapes, diced apple, olives, almonds or pecans are only a few ingredients you might add.
(Experimentation is the key to imaginative salads.)

Serve chicken salad in a scooped-out tomato shell or make a great sandwich.

FRUIT SALAD

Preparation Time: 10 minutes *Serves 4–6*

Nothing is more refreshing in the summer than a fruit salad. Change the fruits with the season.

INGREDIENTS

1 pint strawberries, stemmed and washed
1 pint blueberries, washed
2 oranges, peeled and sliced thin
1 pineapple, peeled and sliced
1 medium avocado, peeled, pitted, and sliced into half-moons
Salad greens

DIRECTIONS

Prepare fruits. Arrange fruits prettily on a platter lined with salad greens.
Serve salad with lime sauce.

TO MAKE SAUCE

1 8-ounce package cream cheese, at room temperature
1/3 cup sugar
1/4 cup fresh lime juice
2 tablespoons milk

In a small bowl beat cream cheese until smooth.
Beat in sugar, lime juice, and milk until blended.
Serve separately with fruit salad.

DESSERTS

There is one dessert that everyone likes—pie, and of all American pies, apple pie is by actual statistics the most favored dessert. Wonderful high layer cakes with glossy chocolate on their tops or fresh coconut or fruits and nuts between layers are strictly American inventions. Also unique to America is strawberry shortcake with a rich hot biscuit base, heavily buttered, and only in America are there blueberry muffins. Delicious breads abound, such as Boston Brown bread, biscuits, Sally Lunn, and numerous corn breads. And not enough can be said about the desserts learned from the Indians, such as Indian pudding, slow-baked to a quivery jelly, johnnycake or pumpkin stew, the forerunner of our pumpkin pie.

INDIAN PUDDING

Preparation and Cooking Time: 2 hours 30 minutes

Serves 4–6

If there was ever such a thing as a "classic" American dessert, it must be Indian pudding, which Indians taught the early colonists to make. This standard and favorite dessert throughout New England was served in John Adams' home on the first Fourth of July and President Teddy Roosevelt had a great love for it.

INGREDIENTS

4 cups milk, scalded
⅓ cup cornmeal

DIRECTIONS

Scald milk in the top of a double boiler; slowly add cornmeal and cook 25 minutes.

½ cup molasses
1 teaspoon salt
⅓ cup sugar
2 tablespoons butter
¾ teaspoon cinnamon
½ teaspoon nutmeg
½ cup chopped dates,
  chopped figs, or raisins
  (*optional*)
½ cup chopped walnuts
  (*optional*)

Stir frequently.
When cooked, add molasses, salt, sugar, butter, cinnamon, nutmeg, and fruits and/or nuts if desired. Mix together thoroughly.
Pour mixture into a greased baking dish and bake in a 275° F. oven for 2 hours.

AUNT ROSIE'S RICE PUDDING

Preparation and Baking Time: 1 hour 15 minutes   Serves 6

A superb basic rice pudding filled with plump raisins which my Aunt Rosie, Mrs. Louis Ronzitti, makes. No dessert no matter how special ever pleased President Grant as much as simple rice pudding.

INGREDIENTS
3 cups milk

3 large eggs, beaten
½ cup sugar
½ teaspoon salt

DIRECTIONS
Scald or heat milk until almost boiling in a saucepan; allow hot milk to cool slightly.

Mix together eggs, sugar, and salt in a 1½-quart baking dish.
Add hot milk slowly, stirring constantly.

1 cup cooked rice
1 teaspoon vanilla
½ cup raisins

Stir in cooked rice, vanilla, and raisins.
Place baking dish in a pan containing one inch of hot water in oven.
Bake at 350° F. for 1 hour or until set. Stir once after pudding has been in the oven about 15 minutes.

BREAD PUDDING

Preparation and Baking Time: 45 minutes *Serves 4–6*

Americans inherit the English enjoyment of puddings. The early settlers of New England ate puddings as a first course.

INGREDIENTS

3 large eggs
½ teaspoon lemon juice
½ teaspoon vanilla
1 cup sugar

DIRECTIONS

Blend eggs, lemon juice, vanilla, and sugar together in a large mixing bowl.

1 cup milk
1 cup light cream
Dash or two of nutmeg

Add milk, light cream, and nutmeg; mix thoroughly.

5 slices dry white bread, broken into small pieces
¾ cup raisins
2 tablespoons butter

Place bread pieces in a casserole and pour liquid mixture over it.
Add raisins and mix gently. Top with dots of butter and another sprinkling of nutmeg.

Bake at 350° F. for 30–35 minutes or until golden brown.

Let pudding rest at room temperature 30 minutes before serving.

VARIATIONS

Instead of raisins, add ½ cup shredded coconut or 1 teaspoon grated lemon rind and a dash of cinnamon.

OZARK PUDDING

Preparation and Baking Time: 45 minutes   *Serves 6*

Here is a wonderful southern mountain recipe for a no-crust pie from Mrs. Tom (Stephanie) Olivo. Ozark Pudding was introduced to the White House by Mrs. Truman.

INGREDIENTS	**DIRECTIONS**
	Preheat oven to 350° F.; butter well a 9-inch pie pan and set aside.
1 large egg *⅔ cup sugar*	In a medium mixing bowl beat egg until thick and lemon-colored; gradually add sugar to egg mixture while continuing to beat.

⅓ cup flour
¼ teaspoon salt
1½ teaspoons baking powder

Sift flour, salt, and baking powder into egg mixture and stir until well blended.

1 cup peeled, chopped raw apples
½ cup chopped black walnuts or pecans

Fold apples and nuts into batter.

Pour it all into the buttered pie pan.

Bake 30 minutes or until it is golden and crisp. The pudding will fall slightly after baking.

1 cup heavy cream, whipped

Top it off with whipped cream and serve 6 happy people.

PEANUT COOKIES

Preparation and Baking Time: 45 minutes   Makes 2 dozen

These were a favorite in my Grandmother Kuster's home as they are in mine.

INGREDIENTS

DIRECTIONS

Preheat oven to 375° F. and butter two cookie sheets. Set aside.

¼ cup butter
½ cup sugar

In a large mixing bowl cream butter and sugar together.

1 large egg, beaten
2 tablespoons milk

Add egg and milk; stir until well blended.

1 cup flour
¼ teaspoon salt

Sift flour, salt, and baking powder into mixture; stir

1 teaspoon baking powder	until thoroughly blended.
¾ cup ground peanuts	Add peanuts to batter and stir until well mixed.
	Drop cookie mixture by the teaspoon onto greased cookie sheets one inch apart.
	Bake for 10 minutes or until a light golden brown.

COCONUT-BUTTER COOKIES

Preparation Time: 15 minutes   *Makes 6–7 dozen*
(*Does not include refrigeration or baking time.*)

Slice-and-bake cookies such as these are perfect for unexpected company.

INGREDIENTS	DIRECTIONS
½ pound butter, at room temperature	Cream butter with fork or wire whisk, gradually adding sugar.
¾ cup sugar	
2 eggs	Add eggs, orange juice, and vanilla; beat until well mixed.
2 tablespoons orange juice	
1 teaspoon vanilla	
	Set aside.
3 cups flour	Sift together flour, baking powder, and baking soda.
1 teaspoon baking powder	
¾ teaspoon baking soda	Gradually stir flour mixture into butter-and-egg mixture.
	Set aside.

¾ cup flaked coconut	Grate or rub the coconut between your fingers to break it up into tiny pieces.
	Mix the coconut into the cookie dough.
	Divide dough into 6 parts; roll each part into a rope 1 inch in diameter.
	Wrap each roll in wax paper and refrigerate overnight or longer.
	(The cookie dough can be frozen at this point if you don't plan to bake them the next day.)
	To bake, preheat oven to 375° F. and lightly grease cookie sheets.
	Slice dough ⅛-inch thick and place 1 inch apart on cookie sheets.
	Bake about 8 minutes or until done. Watch closely.

BROWNIES

Preparation and Baking Time: 40 minutes

Makes 2–2½ dozen

Brownies can be mixed together in the same saucepan used to melt the chocolate and butter.

INGREDIENTS	DIRECTIONS
	Preheat oven to 350° F. and grease a 9-inch-square pan.

2½ (1-ounce) squares unsweetened chocolate
¼ pound butter, at room temperature

Melt the chocolate and butter together in a large saucepan over low heat, stirring constantly.

Remove melted chocolate mixture from heat and allow to cool slightly.

1 cup sugar
2 large eggs
½ cup flour
⅛ teaspoon salt
1 teaspoon vanilla
½ cup chopped walnuts or pecans

Add sugar and eggs to cooled chocolate mixture; beat together until well mixed.

Blend in flour and salt until thoroughly mixed.

Add vanilla and nuts and stir thoroughly.

Spread batter in bottom of greased pan; bake 20–25 minutes.

Cool in pan before cutting into squares or bars.

COFFEE ICE CREAM PIE

Preparation Time: 30 minutes
(Does not include freezing time.)

Makes one 9-inch pie

Simple, but so good. Chocolate and almonds are hidden under the ice cream.

INGREDIENTS
½ gallon coffee ice cream

DIRECTIONS
Let ice cream soften slightly at room temperature while you are preparing the crust and

filling so that it will spread easily.

TO MAKE CRUST

1¼ *cups graham cracker crumbs (15 to 17)*
¼ *cup sugar*
¼ *cup butter or margarine, at room temperature*

Graham cracker crumbs are available in packages. Or you can make them in a jiffy by blending the crackers in an electric blender. If you crush the crackers, place them in a plastic bag or between sheets of wax paper before using the rolling pin.

In a medium bowl combine crumbs with sugar and butter; mix thoroughly until crumbly.

Press mixture firmly against sides and bottom of pie pan. Refrigerate until ready to use.

TO MAKE FILLING

2 *6-ounce almond chocolate bars, broken into pieces*
½ *cup hot water*
1 *tablespoon instant coffee*

Place chocolate and hot water in a small saucepan; melt chocolate over medium heat, stirring constantly.

When melted, remove from heat and stir in coffee.

Set aside to cool slightly.

To assemble pie, pour three fourths of melted chocolate into crust.

Spread ice cream over the top. Dribble the remaining

chocolate on top. Place in freezer for four hours, or overnight.

Remove from freezer about 30 minutes before serving.

VARIATIONS

There is no limit to the number of ice cream pies you can devise.

Fill a crumb crust with peach ice cream and at serving time garnish with sweetened blueberries or strawberries and whipped cream. Or how about lemon sherbet with sweetened, sliced peaches.

MOM'S APPLE PIE

Preparation and Baking Time: 1 hour 30 minutes
Makes one 9-inch pie

Statistics show that apple pie is by far the favorite of all American pies. My mother makes the best apple pie I've ever had.

INGREDIENTS	DIRECTIONS
TO MAKE PASTRY FOR TWO-CRUST PIE	
2 cups sifted flour	Combine flour, salt, and shortening in a large mixing bowl.
1 teaspoon salt	
¾ cup shortening	
	Cut in shortening with a pastry blender or with two knives

	until mixture is consistency of coarse cornmeal.
4–5 tablespoons cold water	Sprinkle on cold water, one tablespoon at a time, tossing mixture lightly and stirring with a fork.

The dough should be just moist enough to hold together when pressed gently into a ball. It should not be sticky.

Divide dough in half and shape each piece into a smooth ball with your hands.

Place one dough ball on a lightly floured surface and press with hand in a flat circle.

Roll dough lightly with short strokes from center in all directions to ⅛-inch thickness.

Fold rolled dough in half and ease it loosely into pie pan with fold in center.

Unfold and fit into pan, being careful not to stretch dough.

Gently press out air pockets with finger tips.

Trim edge even with pie pan.

Roll second ball like the first one for bottom crust and fold.

Cover and reserve.

TO MAKE FILLING

¾ cup sugar or more depending on tartness of apples
2 tablespoons flour
¾ teaspoon cinnamon
6 cups (approximately 2½ pounds) sliced, peeled, tart apples, sliced ¼-inch thick in half-moons
2 tablespoons butter

Mix sugar, flour, and cinnamon together.
Put half of mixture on bottom of pie shell.
Top with half the apples.
Sprinkle with rest of mixture; top with rest of apples.
Dot with butter. (If you wish, you can combine apples and sugar mixture and place in pie shell at one time.)
Gently unfold reserved pie dough over top of pie.
Trim with scissors or knife to ½ inch beyond edge of pie.
Fold top edge under bottom crust edge and press gently with fingers to seal.
Crimp edge as desired.
Cut vents in top crust or prick with fork to allow steam to escape.
(Or cut vents before placing pastry on top of pie.)
Bake in a hot 400° F. oven 50–60 minutes or until crust is brown and apples bubbly.

VARIATIONS

To make a one-crust pie, proceed in the same way but

use half the ingredients: 1 cup sifted flour, ½ teaspoon salt, ⅓ cup plus 1 tablespoon shortening and approximately 2–2½ tablespoons cold water.

Once you learn to make pie crust, you can make any pie you want.

PUMPKIN PIE

Preparation and Baking Time: 1 hour   Makes one 9-inch pie

A must for Thanksgiving dinner. A perfect pumpkin pie is one of the real additions made by American cookery to the good things of the world.

INGREDIENTS	DIRECTIONS
	Preheat oven to 400° F.
1¼ cups cooked or canned pumpkin ¾ cup sugar ½ teaspoon salt ¼ teaspoon ginger ⅛ teaspoon nutmeg 1 teaspoon cinnamon 1 teaspoon flour	Place pumpkin, sugar, salt, ginger, nutmeg, cinnamon, and flour in a large mixing bowl. Mix well.
2 large eggs, slightly beaten	Add eggs and stir until blended.
1 cup evaporated milk 2 tablespoons water ½ teaspoon vanilla	Add milk, water, and vanilla; stir until well mixed.

1 9-inch unbaked pie shell

Pour into unbaked pie shell.
Bake 45–50 minutes or until knife inserted in center comes out clean.
Serve with whipped cream if desired.

LEMON CHESS PIE

Preparation and Baking Time: 45 minutes

Makes one 9-inch pie

(*Doesn't include time to make a pie shell.*)

Chess pies, which are relatively inexpensive to make, are of English origin. They are extremely popular in the South. Here's how to make lemon and chocolate chess pies.

INGREDIENTS

2 cups sugar
1 tablespoon flour
1 tablespoon cornmeal

4 large eggs
¼ cup melted butter
¼ cup milk
3 tablespoons grated lemon rind
¼ cup fresh lemon juice

1 9-inch unbaked pie shell

DIRECTIONS

Combine sugar, flour, and cornmeal in a large mixing bowl; toss lightly with a fork.

Add eggs, butter, milk, lemon rind, and lemon juice.
Beat until smooth and thoroughly blended.

Pour in unbaked pie shell and bake 35–40 minutes at 350° F. or until top is golden brown.

VARIATIONS

This chocolate chess pie recipe is just too good not to mention. Bake pie shell at 475° F. 3 minutes. Set aside. Melt together ¼ pound butter with 1½ squares unsweetened chocolate.

Mix 1 cup brown sugar, ½ cup white sugar and 1 tablespoon flour together and add to butter mixture. Beat together 2 eggs, ½ eggshellful of milk, and 1 teaspoon vanilla together; stir into sugar mixture.

Pour into pie shell; bake at 325° F. for 35–40 minutes until set.

STRAWBERRY SHORTCAKE

Preparation and Baking Time: 30 minutes   Makes 8 biscuits

Strawberry shortcake has been popular in America since the colonists first discovered strawberries. Old-fashioned shortcake is always made with biscuit dough, not cake.

INGREDIENTS

DIRECTIONS
Preheat oven to 350° F. and grease a cookie sheet.

1 quart fresh strawberries,
  hulled and washed
Sugar to taste

TO MAKE BISCUITS
2 cups flour
2 tablespoons sugar
½ teaspoon salt
2 teaspoons baking powder
3 tablespoons shortening

1 egg
¼ cup milk

Butter
Heavy cream (*optional*)

Crush strawberries slightly and sweeten to taste. Set aside.

Sift together flour, sugar, salt, and baking powder in a medium mixing bowl.
Blend shortening into dry ingredients with a pastry blender.
Beat egg and milk together.
Stir in, little by little, egg mixture into other ingredients until dough holds together but is still soft.
Turn out on a floured board and divide into 8 parts. Pat or roll out. Place on cookie sheet.
Bake 20 minutes or until golden brown.

Split hot biscuits with a fork; spread lightly with butter; put fruit between layers and on top.
Serve with unsweetened heavy cream, unwhipped.

VARIATIONS
Raspberries, blueberries, peaches, and apricots are delicious too.

TRIFLE

Preparation Time: 15 minutes *Serves 4–6*
(*Does not include chilling time.*)

The trifle was brought to America by the British colonists.

INGREDIENTS

1 small jellyroll
⅓ cup orange juice
½ teaspoon rum flavoring

1 3-ounce package vanilla or banana pudding
1 teaspoon vanilla

1 1-pound can fruit cocktail, drained
1 banana, peeled and sliced

1 cup heavy cream, whipped
¼ cup toasted, slivered, blanched almonds
8 maraschino cherries, halved

DIRECTIONS

Slice jellyroll and place slices cut side down in a pretty serving dish.

Sprinkle jellyroll with orange juice and rum flavoring.

Refrigerate while preparing pudding.

Prepare pudding according to the directions on the package.

Stir vanilla into pudding.

Cool pudding.

Spread drained fruit cocktail on top of sliced jellyroll; then add the sliced banana and finally spread the pudding on top.

Refrigerate at least 4 hours before serving.

When ready to serve, spread whipped cream over the top of the pudding; then sprinkle with almonds and cherries.

Serve immediately.

VARIATIONS

Instead of using a jelly roll, it is traditional to use sponge cake and spread this with ⅓ cup raspberry preserves.

BOSTON CREAM PIE

Preparation and Baking Time: 45 minutes

Makes one 8-inch cake

(Does not include chilling time.)

Boston cream pie is actually a cake filled with custard and topped with confectioners' sugar or chocolate icing.

INGREDIENTS
TO MAKE CAKE

1 large egg
½ cup sugar
1½ tablespoons melted butter

½ cup plus 2 tablespoons flour
1 teaspoon baking powder
Pinch of salt

6 tablespoons milk
Dash of lemon juice

DIRECTIONS

Preheat oven to 375° F. and line bottom of 8-inch cake pan with wax paper. Set aside. Beat egg in mixing bowl until light; gradually add the sugar.
When well blended, add melted butter.

Sift the flour, baking powder, and salt together.

Add flour mixture alternately with milk to egg batter until well blended.

Flavor with lemon. Mix thoroughly.
Pour batter into cake pan.
Bake for 20–25 minutes.
Remove from pan and pull off the paper.
Cool.

TO MAKE FILLING

1 small package vanilla pudding

Prepare vanilla pudding according to package directions, using only 1¾ cups milk.
Cover and chill. Beat until fluffy and smooth.
When the cake is thoroughly cool, split and fill with vanilla pudding between layers.
Sift a little confectioners' sugar on the top or top with chocolate icing.

TO MAKE ICING

4 ounces semisweet or sweet chocolate
1 tablespoon butter
3 tablespoons water

Melt the chocolate and butter with water over boiling water; remove from heat.

1 cup confectioners' sugar
Pinch of salt
½ teaspoon vanilla

Combine sugar and salt; add to chocolate mixture gradually, blending thoroughly. Stir in vanilla. Spread evenly over top of the cake.

VARIATIONS

Washington cream pie is made with the same cake.

Just fill with raspberry jam, omitting the custard filling.

Sprinkle the top with confectioners' sugar.

CHOCOLATE ICE BOX CAKE

Preparation Time: 20 minutes *Makes one 10-inch cake*
(*Does not include chilling time.*)

Ice box cakes such as this delicious chocolate one require very little time or experience to make. Make it the night before at your leisure.

INGREDIENTS

3 4-ounce German Sweet chocolate bars
3 tablespoons hot water

DIRECTIONS

Melt chocolate in water in a double boiler or in a medium saucepan over low heat.

If melted in a saucepan, watch carefully that it does not burn. Stir frequently.

Remove melted chocolate from heat and cool.

6 medium eggs, separated
3 tablespoons sugar
1½ teaspoons vanilla

Beat egg yolks in a large mixing bowl until lemon-colored; gradually add sugar.

Stir in chocolate and finally the vanilla.

	Set aside.
1 cup heavy cream, whipped	Beat egg whites until stiff. Fold beaten egg whites and whipped cream into chocolate mixture. Reserve.
3 dozen lady fingers	Line bottom and sides of a lightly greased 10-inch cake spring mold with lady fingers. Pour in 1/3 of chocolate mixture; top with a few lady fingers. Repeat until all of the ingredients are used up, ending with the chocolate mixture. Refrigerate overnight. This cake can be frozen if you like. Remove at least 30 minutes before serving.

GRANDMOTHER KUSTER'S APPLESAUCE CAKE

Preparation and Baking Time: 45 minutes

Makes one 10-inch-square cake

Applesauce cakes are extremely economical and they keep moist for days. This is my grandmother's recipe.

INGREDIENTS	DIRECTIONS
	Preheat oven to 350° F. and grease a 10-inch-square pan. Set aside.
½ cup shortening 1 cup brown sugar	Cream shortening with sugar until fluffy in a large mixing bowl.
3 large eggs	Add eggs and beat thoroughly.
2 cups flour 1½ teaspoons baking soda 1 teaspoon cinnamon	Sift flour, baking soda, and cinnamon together.
1½ cups applesauce 2 tablespoons black molasses	Mix applesauce with black molasses; then add applesauce mixture alternately with dry ingredients to egg mixture. Beat well after each addition.
2 cups raisins	Add raisins and stir well. Pour into greased 10-inch-square pan and bake about 30 minutes.

NOBBY APPLE CAKE

Preparation and Baking Time: 1 hour

Makes one 10-inch-square cake

Apples were a favorite ingredient in days past because they could be kept all winter long in cold cellars for delicious cakes like this one from Mrs. Dan (Dorothy) Wargo.

INGREDIENTS

½ cup butter or margarine, at room temperature
1 cup sugar
1 large egg, beaten

1 cup flour
½ teaspoon baking soda
½ teaspoon cinnamon
½ teaspoon salt

3 cups diced raw apples
½ cup raisins or ½ cup chopped walnuts or pecans (*optional*)

TO MAKE HARD SAUCE

⅓ cup butter, at room temperature
1 cup confectioners' sugar, sifted
¾ teaspoon vanilla or 2 tablespoons orange juice and 2 tablespoons grated orange rind or 2 tablespoons brandy, rum, or sherry

DIRECTIONS

Preheat oven to 350° F.
Grease a 10-inch-square cake pan. Set aside.
Cream butter and sugar in a large mixing bowl; add egg and mix thoroughly.

Sift flour, baking soda, cinnamon, and salt together.
Add to mixing bowl and stir until well blended.

Add apples and raisins or nuts; mix well.
Pour into greased cake pan; bake 40–45 minutes.
Serve warm or cold with or without whipped cream, ice cream, or hard sauce.

Cream butter thoroughly.
Add sugar and beat in gradually until light and fluffy.
Continue beating and add flavoring. The perfect sauce should be fluffy and smooth.

POOR MAN'S CAKE

Preparation and Baking Time: 45 minutes

Makes one 9 by 13-inch cake

Plump raisins are the secret of this very moist cake. As a kid in the Midwest Mrs. Lou (Joanne) Starkey loved this cake with a big glass of milk.

INGREDIENTS	DIRECTIONS
	Preheat oven to 350° F. and grease a 9 by 13-inch cake pan. Set aside.
1 tablespoon flour 1½ cups water 1 cup raisins	Dissolve the flour in a little water in a small saucepan. Add rest of water and raisins; bring to a boil for a minute or so. Remove from heat and allow to cool.
1 cup sugar ½ cup shortening 1 teaspoon baking soda 1 tablespoon cold water 1 large egg, beaten	Cream sugar and shortening together in a mixing bowl. Set aside. Dissolve baking soda in water; then add with beaten egg to sugar mixture.
1½ cups flour 1 teaspoon cinnamon 1 teaspoon allspice 1 teaspoon cloves	Sift flour and spices into sugar mixture; add raisin mixture and mix until well blended. Pour into greased cake pan. Bake 20–25 minutes.

Powdered sugar

Sprinkle while warm with powdered sugar.
This cake is even better the second day.

SOUR CREAM COFFEE CAKE

Preparation and Baking Time: 1 hour   Makes one loaf cake

Delicious choice for Sunday morning breakfast. It's easy to make.

INGREDIENTS

½ cup butter, at room temperature
1 cup sugar
2 large eggs
1 teaspoon vanilla

2 cups sifted flour
1½ teaspoons baking powder
1 teaspoon baking soda
¼ teaspoon salt
1 cup sour cream

½ cup chopped walnuts or pecans
½ cup sugar

DIRECTIONS

Preheat oven to 350° F.
Grease tube or loaf pan. Set aside.
Cream together butter and sugar in a large mixing bowl.
Add eggs and vanilla; beat well.

Sift together flour, baking powder, baking soda and salt.
Add dry ingredients alternately with sour cream, beginning and ending with dry ingredients. Mix well.

In a separate bowl mix together nuts, sugar, and cinnamon.

1 teaspoon cinnamon

Pour half the batter into greased tube pan.
Sprinkle half of the nut mixture on top.
Pour remaining batter over the top.
Sprinkle top with rest of nut mixture.
Bake about 50 minutes.

VARIATIONS
Put chocolate chips in center of batter.

BOSTON BROWN BREAD

Preparation and Baking Time: 2 hours 15 minutes

Makes 5 small loaves

A dark brown steamed bread made with cornmeal and sweetened with molasses, this was popular in New England during Colonial times.

INGREDIENTS

1 cup cornmeal
1 cup whole-wheat flour
1 cup white flour
1 teaspoon salt
1 teaspoon baking soda

1¾ cups milk
1 cup molasses
1 cup raisins

DIRECTIONS

Sift cornmeal, flour, salt, and baking soda together in a large bowl.

Add milk and molasses; stir until blended.
Mix in raisins.

Pour into greased cans ⅔ full and cover with aluminum foil.
Place cans in pan containing at least 1 inch of water.
Steam two hours in a 375° F. oven.
Remove from cans.
(This recipe makes five cans if soup cans are used.)

HOE CAKES

Preparation and Cooking Time: 15 minutes *Serves 4*

A favorite breakfast of George Washington, an early riser, was Indian hoe cakes, honey, and tea. Hoe cakes, typical southern colonial fare, were originally baked right on a hoe in the open hearth and were commonly served with vegetable soup. By the way, soup was a typical breakfast dish of the time.

INGREDIENTS
1 cup white cornmeal
1 teaspoon salt
2 tablespoons bacon fat or oil
Boiling water

DIRECTIONS
Combine cornmeal with the salt in mixing bowl.
Add bacon fat and enough boiling water a little at a time to make a dough that is solid enough to hold a shape.
Form into little cakes the size of a silver dollar.

Bacon fat or oil

Fry cakes in hot bacon fat or oil until browned on both sides.
Serve hot.

JOHNNYCAKE

Preparation and Baking Time: 40 minutes

Makes one 8-inch-square cake

Johnnycake is a corruption of journey cake, a hard biscuit that could easily be carried on a long trip. Popular at breakfast or as a dessert at Sunday night supper with maple syrup.

INGREDIENTS

2 cups cornmeal
½ cup flour
1 teaspoon baking soda
1 teaspoon baking powder

½ cup sugar
2 large eggs
2 tablespoons melted butter
1 cup sour milk

DIRECTIONS

Sift cornmeal, flour, baking soda, and baking powder together in large mixing bowl.

Mix sugar with beaten egg.
Add egg mixture, melted butter and sour milk to flour mixture.
Beat up quickly and bake in a well-buttered 8 by 8-inch pan for 25–30 minutes in a 375° F. oven.
Serve with plenty of butter.

BLUEBERRY MUFFINS

Preparation and Baking Time: 30 minutes *Makes 12*

Blueberries in their wild state are found from the northern tip of Alaska down to Florida, and have always been eaten by Indians. Blueberry muffins are an American invention.

INGREDIENTS

1¾ cups sifted flour
¼ cup sugar
2½ teaspoons baking powder
¾ teaspoon salt

1 large egg, beaten
¾ cup milk
⅓ cup melted shortening
1 cup fresh or well-drained frozen blueberries

DIRECTIONS

Preheat oven to 400° F.
Grease muffin pan and set aside.
Sift together dry ingredients; make a well in the center.

Combine egg, milk, and shortening in center; stir quickly only until dry ingredients are moistened.
Gently stir blueberries into batter.
Fill greased muffin pan ⅔ full.
Bake 25 minutes or until done.

WHAT EVERY KITCHEN NEEDS

FOR PREPARATION
Can Opener
Colander
Cutlery Set (butcher knife, 7- or 8-inch blade; bread knife, serrated blade; 2 paring knives)
Cutting Board
Grater
Kitchen Scissors
Vegetable Brush
Vegetable Peeler

FOR COOKING
Double Boiler (1½ quarts)
Frying Pans (6 and 10 inches)
Pancake Turner
Saucepans (1 quart, 3 quarts, and 4 to 6 quarts)

FOR MIXING
Flour Sifter
Kitchen Fork and Knife
Mixing Bowls

Pastry Blender
Rotary Egg Beater or Electric Mixer
Rubber Scraper
Wooden Spoon

FOR MEASURING

Graduated Measuring Cups (¼, ⅓, ½, 1 cup)
Liquid Measuring Cup
Measuring Spoons (¼, ½, 1 teaspoon, 1 tablespoon)

FOR BAKING

Baking Sheet
Loaf Pan (9 inches)
Muffin Pan (12 cups)
Oblong pan (12 inches)
Pastry Cloth
Pie Pan
Rolling Pin
Round Layer Pans (2) (8 or 9 inches)
Spatula
Square Pans (2) (8 and 10 inches)
Wire Rack

WEIGHTS AND MEASURES

Dash=less than ⅛ teaspoon

4 quarts (solid)=1 peck

3 teaspoons=1 tablespoon

4 pecks=1 bushel

4 tablespoons=¼ cup

16 ounces=1 pound

5⅓ tablespoons=⅓ cup

8 tablespoons=½ cup

16 tablespoons=1 cup

2 tablespoons=1 liquid ounce

1 cup=½ pint

2 cups=1 pint

2 pints (4 cups)=1 quart

4 quarts (liquid)=1 gallon

GLOSSARY OF COOKING TERMS

Bake Cook in oven.
Beat Mix vigorously with a spoon or fork or beater.
Blend Combine two or more ingredients.
Boil Cook in liquid so hot that it bubbles and keeps on bubbling.
Broil Cook next to heat, under broiler in range or over coals.
Chop Cut into pieces with knife or chopper.
Combine Mix together.
Condiments Something served with a food to give additional flavor, such as mustard.
Convenience Foods Foods, such as canned soups, which save time or simplify cooking.
Cream To work to a smooth, creamy mass.
Cube Cut in ¼-inch to ½-inch cubes.
Cut In Combine shortening and flour with pastry blender.
Dice Cut into ¼-inch cubes.
Dot Drop bits of butter or cheese here and there over food.
Drain Pour off liquid.
Flour Dust greased pans with flour until well coated on bottom and sides. Shake out extra flour.
Fold Combine gently until blended.

Grease Spread bottom and sides of pan with shortening.

Knead Work dough with your hands in a folding-back and pressing-forward motion.

Melt Heat until liquid.

Mince Chop into tiny pieces.

Roll Out Place on board and spread thin with a rolling pin.

Shred Cut into very thin strips.

Sift Put through a flour sifter or fine sieve.

Simmer Cook over heat near boiling but not hot enough to bubble.

Soft Shortening Butter, lard, or vegetable shortening at room temperature so it can be measured easily.

Stir Mix round and round with spoon.

Toss Mix lightly.

Whip Add air by beating with beater or electric mixer.

INDEX

Apple Cake, Nobby, 119
Apple Cider, Hot Spiced, 69
Apple Pie, Mom's, 107
Applesauce Cake, Grandmother Kuster's, 118
Arroz con Pollo, 39

Beans
  Boston Baked Beans, 6
  U. S. Senate Bean Soup, 80
Beef
  Hamburgers, Peanut Butter, 83
  Hot Dogs, Classy, 85
  Sauerbraten, 32
  Shepherd's Pie, 28
  Shish Kebab, 63
  Spaghetti with Meat Balls, 40
  Tostados, 22
Beverages
  Apple Cider, Hot Spiced, 69
  Eggnog, 75
Blueberry Muffins, 126
Boston Baked Beans, 6
Boston Brown Bread, 123
Boston Cream Pie, 115

Bread Pudding, 100
Breads
  Blueberry Muffins, 126
  Boston Brown Bread, 123
  Hoe Cakes, 124
  Irish Soda Bread, 60
  Italian Garlic Bread, 40
  Johnnycake, 125
Brownies, 104
Brunswick Stew, 15

Cakes
  Apple Cake, Nobby, 119
  Applesauce Cake, Grandmother Kuster's, 118
  Boston Cream Pie, 115
  Cherry Cobbler, 56
  Chocolate Ice Box Cake, 117
  Fruit Cake, 74
  Gingerbread with Lemon Sauce, 52
  Poor Man's Cake, 121
  Sour Cream Coffee Cake, 122
  Strawberry Shortcake, 112
  Trifle, 114

Candy
  Chocolate-dipped Orange
    Peel, 52
  Popcorn Balls, Halloween, 68
Cherry Cobbler, 56
Chicken. *See* Poultry
Chicken Cordon Bleu, 61
Chicken-Corn Chowder, 82
Chicken Salad, Best Ever, 95
Chicken Tetrazzini, 50
Chicken with Herbed
  Dumplings, 19
Chocolate Chess Pie, 111
Chocolate-dipped Orange Peel,
  52
Chocolate Ice Box Cake, 117
Chopped Liver, 89
Chow Mein, Pork, 90
Cioppino, 24
Clam Chowder, New England,
  10
Coconut-Butter Cookies, 103
Codfish Cakes, 9
Coffee Ice Cream Pie, 105
Cookies
  Brownies, 104
  Coconut-Butter, 103
  Peanut, 102
Cornish Hens with Rice
  Stuffing, 57
Cranberry-Orange Relish, 73
Cucumber Salad, 48

Deviled Eggs, 67

Egg-Lemon Soup with Meat
  Balls, Greek, 43
Eggnog, 75

Fish. *See* Seafood
Fried Rice, Pork, 91
Fruit Cake, 74
Fruit Salad, 96

Gazpacho, 37
Gingerbread with Lemon Sauce
  52
Greek Egg-Lemon Soup with
  Meat Balls, 43

Ham
  Ham Hocks and Collard
    Greens, 13
  Ham and Asparagus Soufflé,
    30
  Jambalaya, 17
  Schnitz Un Knepp, 11
Hoe Cakes, 124
Hot Dogs, Classy, 85

Indian Pudding, 98
Irish Soda Bread, 60
Italian Garlic Bread, 40

Jambalaya, 17
Johnnycake, 125

Lamb: Shish Kebab, 63
Lemon Chess Pie, 111
Liver, Chopped, 89

Neapolitan Casserole, 93

Orange Peel, Chocolate-dipped,
  52
Ozark Pudding, 101

Peanut Butter Hamburgers, 83
Peanut Cookies, 102
Pea Soup, Split, 81
Philadelphia Pepper Pot Soup, 78
Pies
  Apple Pie, Mom's, 107
  Chocolate Chess, 111
  Coffee Ice Cream, 105
  Lemon Chess, 111
  Pumpkin, 110
Pie Crust, 107
Pizza, 85
Poor Man's Cake, 121
Popcorn Balls, Halloween, 68
Pork
  Chow Mein, 90
  Fried Rice, 91
  Schnitz Un Knepp, 11
  Swedish Meat Balls, 35
Potato Dumplings, 34
Potato Salad, 66
Poultry
  Arroz con Pollo, 39
  Chicken Cordon Bleu, 61
  Chicken Salad, Best Ever, 95
  Chicken Tetrazzini, 50
  Chicken with Herbed Dumplings, 19
  Cornish Hens with Rice Stuffing, 57
  Liver, Chopped, 89
  Neapolitan Casserole, 93
  Turkey, Roast, 70
Pudding
  Bread, 100
  Indian, 98
  Ozark, 101

Rice, Aunt Rosie's, 99
Pumpkin Pie, 110

Relish, Cranberry-Orange, 73
Rice
  Arroz con Pollo, 39
  Fried Rice, Pork, 91
  Jambalaya, 17
  Pudding, Aunt Rosie's, 99
  Stuffing, Cornish Hens with, 57

Salads
  Cucumber, 48
  Fruit, 96
  Potato, 66
  Waldorf, 59
Sauerbraten, 32
Schnitz Un Knepp, 11
Seafood
  Cioppino, 24
  Codfish Cakes, 9
  Tempura, 45
  Tuna Fish Casserole, 92
Shepherd's Pie, 28
Shish Kebab, Lamb, Beef, 63
Soufflé, Ham and Asparagus, 30
Soup
  Bean Soup, U. S. Senate, 80
  Chicken-Corn Chowder, 82
  Clam Chowder, New England, 10
  Egg-Lemon Soup with Meat Balls, Greek, 43
  Gazpacho, 37
  Pea Soup, Split, 81
  Philadelphia Pepper Pot Soup, 78

Sour Cream Coffee Cake, 122
Spaghetti with Meat Balls, 40
Stew
   Brunswick Stew, 15
   Cioppino, 24
Strawberry Shortcake, 112
Stuffings
   Rice, with Cornish Hens, 57
   Sausage-Bread, 70
Swedish Meat Balls, 35

Tempura, 45
Tostados, 22
Trifle, 114
Tuna Fish Casserole, 92
Turkey, Roast, 70

U. S. Senate Bean Soup, 80

Waldorf Salad, 59

BETTY L. TORRE was born on a Michigan farm. Her mother loved cooking so the interest came to her naturally. She believes that cooking creatively is a basic part of life and is always collecting favorite recipes from friends and relatives or inventing new ones herself.

She worked for ten years in publishing, most recently as Director of Promotion and Publicity for Ballantine Books. She left publishing to raise a family and presently lives in Northport, Long Island, with her sons and her husband, Frank.

641.5 Torre, Betty L
T   It's easy to cook favorite
       American recipes

DATE DUE	BORROWER'S NAME	

Independent School District #487
Upsala, Minnesota 56384

641.5 Torre, Betty L
T   It's easy to cook favorite
       American recipes